The Gospel According to Molly
From Devil Dog to Sidewalk Saint

David C. Craig

Scripture taken from the New King James Version. Copyright © 1982 by Thomas Nelson, Inc. Used by permission. All rights reserved.

Other Scripture quotations are KJV, King James Version of the Bible

ISBN-10: 1490554254
ISBN-13: 978-1490554259

DEDICATION

This book is dedicated to my Beloved Bride, Jacque, whose love and support undergirded the writing process and whose limitless patience and grace enabled me to both get and keep Molly, once known by all as "Devil Dog".

CONTENTS

ACKNOWLEDGMENTS

I want to thank Pete Karas for all he has done to bring this
book from manuscript to your hands.
I also want to thank my brother Larry for his support in making
this book move from my heart to your home. He is a bibliophile
by passion and a bookseller by trade. He said this book should
be on the market for all to read. Based on his passion and trade,
that was a great encouragement.

CHAPTER ONE

"He spoke many things to them in parables."
Matthew 13:3

A famous line, quoted from somewhere, says simply, "Who loves ya?" Daily humanity, lost and saved alike, asks that question. Who does "love ya?" Daily I ask that question, not randomly or even as a question. As I grab my dog by the ears and rub those baby soft appendages I look her in the eye and exclaim, "Who loves ya! Daddy does!" And she agreeably wags her tail and gives me a slobbery kiss and says in her own doggy language, "Right back at ya!"

This is a parable of love and of all that that love means. It is not just a mushy tale (or tail) of ear rubbing and slobbery kisses, it is a tale of love. I will tell you this up front, I love my dog! And if behavior is any evidence of animal affection, she loves me, too. You may argue, by the way, that animal affection is simply a learned trait for survival, but I am not arguing. This parable isn't about that. It is about me loving my dog and how that simple everyday truth can transform our view of ourselves and the great God who daily loves us.

It may be important at the outset to lay out the parameters of what is a parable. By simplest definition a parable is a story using everyday objects or experiences to relate more clearly a greater truth about God. We cannot get caught up in each detail and fail to see the forest for the trees. A parable is not so much about the details as it is about one clear and concise point.

This truth about parables is essential to understand if we are going to rightly appropriate the truth that Christ is trying to teach us in His parables. I have seen Christians fight, churches split and the name of God blasphemed among the Gentiles over the splitting of hairs on the details of parables. The flip side of this can be and has also been true. When we take the clear teachings of Christ that aren't parables and try to ignore what He is teaching by calling it a parable we engender confusion about doctrine and friction among the brethren. This is, however, a parable.

No picture in it is perfect simply because no one and nothing totally and accurately portrays the matchless perfection of God and His perfect work. The illustrations are designed only for giving a broader picture of a great truth. If we get wrapped up in the illustrations and bicker over them we have doubly stumbled. First we have lost sight of the greater truth which is our main goal. Second we have fallen prey to the evil one and his designs to sow discord in the church, separate the brethren and generally wreak havoc on the advancement of the Christian faith in our lives and in the world.

In short, don't sweat the small stuff. If you disagree with the minutia of an illustration, please look beyond it. This is not about the minutia of an illustration. Put a page marker at this spot and highlight this paragraph. When you get to chapter 5 or 11 or 17 and say, "Wait a minute! That offends me!" look back to this spot. Reread this paragraph and laugh at yourself with that joy of awakened understanding, "Oh, it's not about this (minute detail), it's about that (greater truth)".

I assure you that I am not Christ. My parables are not nearly as good as His. The applications are not perfect and the teaching is limited by human frailty and flesh. It is a parable!

The characters in the parable have feet made of clay or fur.

The greater point is that daily as I interact with my dog (and did I tell you that I love my dog? God teaches me some rich blessings and great lessons that have encouraged me in my walk with Him. They have challenged me to see myself differently and to assess myself more in line of His assessment of me. The grand simplicity of some of the lessons has actually shocked me. "How can this be true of me? Am I really as dumb as my dog?" (This is especially shocking in light of the fact that dogs are much smarter than sheep and God calls us sheep. That reality is embarrassing.)

Now you have met the major players in the drama of this parable. There is me. My role is divine. (Now don't object already – I am not divine. That is just my role. I don't exactly fulfill it perfectly – go figure – right!?) Molly on the other hand is me. Not the divine me, the human me. She is the true man. Please be patient. Yes, she is a girl dog, but I don't have a boy dog so a girl dog will have to represent everyman. Besides, I love my dog and she can grow up to be whatever she wants. This is, after all, the land of the free and the home of way too many spoiled dogs. They have been issued credit cards and signed up to vote. Certainly she can represent every man.

Molly actually is a wonderful dog. She is not officially papered, unless you consider the papers in the corner of the basement to be official. Someone said she looks like a border collie, but her markings are really more like a Karelian Bear Dog. I don't know what Karelian Bear Dogs do, but Molly seems to have the instincts of a border collie. She loves to herd things. Since we have no sheep (at least not of the four footed kind) she is left to herd whatever she finds. That generally includes our grandchildren, who actually don't like to be herded, and our cats who like to be herded even less.

Her solution to that is to grab them by the nape of the neck, the cats – not our grandchildren, and carry them where she wants them to be. While she goes in search of a second victim, the first is quickly gone into safe hiding. This is the type of frustration that only a very patient dog or mother of toddlers can deal with every day and keep on going. (I didn't say that mothers of toddlers grab their offspring by the nape of their necks or that toddlers are the victims of their mother's pursuits, but mothers of toddlers clearly know what I mean.)

This just illustrates that Molly and people have things in common. Goals of life are not always realized. Complications and frustrations arise. Is there here any place for divine interaction or action? Is there any place for people to act divinely? Can the parable have a point? Those are the types of realities that we deal with in the smallest of ways each day. They are situations that can teach so much but can be so quickly overlooked or missed in the rush of life. Molly says, "Slow down and take me for a walk." In slowing down with Molly we can learn a lot.

This is indeed a commandment of the Scriptures. Deuteronomy 6:7 says "And you shall teach them diligently to your children, and shall talk of them when you sit in your house, and when you walk by the way, and when you lie down, and when you rise." (RSV) We are commanded to observe the work of God in our surroundings and to relate that truth to our children. We are commanded to look for God, His nature, His work, His grace, His love and His judgment in all that we find around us. We are commanded to seek and identify illustrations of Him to relate to our children so that they might know Him more clearly and serve Him more correctly.

Every moment is a teachable moment for children. We didn't miss the last great teachable moment yesterday and won't have another one come around until the next sighting of Haley's Comet. No, teachable moments, God says, are everywhere and every day. Life is an ongoing resource for lessons, for parables that make us alert to God and have those "AHA!!" moments when what He is trying to say and do in our lives becomes more clear.

The psalmist says in Psalm 78:2 "I will open my mouth in a

parable" in order to teach the children of Israel how to teach their children about how great God is. The reality of the psalm is that the generations of Israel had forgotten to obey the commandment in Deuteronomy and had fallen on hard times. They needed a new parable to awaken them to God's truth.

We must find in our surroundings, the environment of our lives, the lessons that will teach us about God. Not only our children, but we adults who are children of God, need to be daily renewed in the finer points of His greatness. As His children it is His desire to teach us and instruct us about Himself. He knows that we are children; certainly compared to Him we are barely toddlers. And so the lessons that we will teach to our children and grandchildren about God will first impact us. We will grow as we look for Him. We will find God greater as we seek to find God more often.

And so Molly says, "Slow down and take me for a walk." It has been on my daily walks with Molly, and we try to go on three walks of one mile each per day, that God has shown me great things. He has brought to my mind and heart great truths wrapped up in the furry friend who is with me. I have pondered things that I don't usually ponder at my desk or when attending to the many duties of the church. God has laid on my heart parables, simple stories, simple illustrations of Himself and me. And while I certainly enjoy my time with Molly, it has also greatly enriched my time with God. Come along with Molly and me on a few walks through life.

CHAPTER TWO

"And preached peace to you who were afar off."
Ephesians 2:17

It was 6:30 in the morning, and I am definitely not a morning person. From the kennel downstairs in the library I heard this persistent whine. Whose dog is that my fogged mind asked? I sure am glad it is **not my dog**.

There are so many things to say here that it is hard to begin. What is the nugget of this parable? Molly is "Not My Dog"!!! That is how it began, or re-began if that is a term at all. Her name was indeed already Molly, but historically speaking, she was not my dog.

Molly was to be quite exact, my historic enemy. She had moved into our house, or at least her kennel in an out of the way space in our house, the night before. That is perhaps part B of this parable because we have to move back in time to before that fateful evening that would change her life for the better.

Molly had been a well-traveled dog for her young life. When she came that late March night to live with us we were in fact her 6th stop on the road of domestic turmoil. She had belonged to her birth home. She had then belonged to another home and then another home after that. Then she became the property of my sons who gave her to my daughter's boyfriend from whom we acquired her. All that was before age one!

I had been acquainted with her for the previous six months of her life prior to coming to my house to stay. I had been acquainted and very glad indeed that she was not my dog. In fact my wife, who will play various roles in these parables, was exceedingly glad that she was not our dog and made it abundantly clear on that fateful March evening that if Molly came to live with us she would continue to be not her dog. That is why I call her my dog. She is after all this time, not my wife's dog. (Liar, liar pants on fire. You should see her with Molly. OK, on some rare occasions you should see her with Molly and you would be mystified at the statement – "She is not her dog". But for all practical purposes, and by the confession of her own lips, Molly is not her dog.)

Molly was also not my dog at one time. She was not my dog in the same sense that we were at one point not God's children. Isaiah 65:1 says, "I was found by those who did not seek Me. I said, 'Here I am, here I am' to a nation that was not called by My Name." Each of us entered this world estranged from God. By birth we are sinners and by birthright separated from Him. It is that simple. We were not God's sheep. We were and are His creation, but it is simple contemporary heresy to say that all people are really just children of God.

II Corinthians 5:18 says, "Now all things are of God, who has reconciled us to Himself through Jesus Christ, and has given us the ministry of reconciliation." That little phrase "through Jesus Christ" cannot be overlooked or omitted. We are only reconciled to God through Christ. If we don't have Christ; if we don't know Him, believe Him or trust Him then we are not reconciled to God.

A missionary friend of mine was chastised by a funeral home in New York City for his omission at a funeral. He had been called in to preside over the funeral of a person who had died without either membership or participation in a church. No personal family clergy were known, so he got the call. He had never met the person and after talking with the family of the deceased was left without any grounds for belief that the departed had ever had even a passing interest in God. At the funeral, therefore, he did not make the grand pronouncement that the departed had already entered their heavenly reward.

This omission approached a scandalous position as far as the funeral home was concerned. I am sure that the family had made comments and the home was passing them along. The world would say that we are all, each and every one of us, children of God and destined for a glory bound road when we die. The world has hopes, great hopes, of getting in there some way or other. As the old spiritual would say, "Ebry body talkin' 'bout heabn ain't goin' there". How true; how very very true!

And why aren't they going? Because they are not God's children if they don't know God's child. Jesus said it in John 5:23, "He who does not honor the Son does not honor the Father who sent Him". (NKJV) In John 14:6 He says, "I Am the Way, the Truth and the Life, no one comes to the Father except through Me". (NKJV) That is what Paul said in II Corinthians 5, "through Jesus Christ". John reiterates this truth in I John 5:12, "He who has the Son has life; he who does not have the Son of God does not have life". (NKJV)

There is just no way around it. We are either God's child or we are not. Not everyone is and there is only way to become so. We come through the Son or we do not come at all. God loved the world so much that He gave His Only Son to die for the sins of man. With the provision He declared that there was never and would never be another way to approach Him. Jesus is the way to God, and those who choose to not come by Jesus are simply not God's children. Hard truth and painful reality that it is; it is God's own word that we have on the topic. When He speaks discussion is effectively ended.

I, at one time was not God's child. Molly was at one time not my dog. Now I am God's child and now Molly is my dog. Simple parable, great truth, exceeding great joy!

But, if I weren't God's child, then whose child was I? I like the Bible a lot because, quite simply, it keeps me from having to make these things up. The answers to the questions are in it. Because we often don't like the answers we pretend they aren't there, but they are.

Jesus made a powerful comment to His Jewish critics. Remember the Jewish people were God's chosen people. They were not some random group of strangers to God. He called and chose Abraham. He extended the promise to Isaac and Jacob and on down the line. In Deuteronomy 7:6 He makes clear that He has chosen them to be His special people. Throughout the prophets He reminds them that they are His people. He watched over them, protected them, provided for them, chastised them when they sinned and restored them when they repented. He did all this because they were His chosen people. But being His chosen people did not make them all His children. (Paul laments over this a great deal in the book of Romans.)

What does Jesus say to this special called group of people? In John 8:44 He says to them, "You are of your father the devil". This was not said to the nation as a whole, but to a group of leaders that rejected both His teachings and Him. He said to them, "If God were your Father, you would love Me". John 8:42. This is a harsh denunciation of a group of people that had very high expectations. To them God said, "You are not my children." If the very descendants of Abraham were not His children apart from faith in His revealed Son, the condition of all mankind is plainly clear. We are a people who were not called by His Name as Isaiah has said. We were not His.

Molly was not mine. She was in fact a dog that I very much hated. She was a terror in every sense of the word. She was a sinner of great proportions. Even her existence in our family was a result of sin. My oldest son's wife is allergic to dogs. She asked him not to get a dog. He and my youngest son went to get a dog anyway. They brought her home and told her they had to do so as they had hit her on the road and took her in to make sure she was OK. (These wicked children must belong to my wife.) My daughter-in-law was not fooled, but yielded to her presence.

One day when my youngest son's fiancée was visiting at my oldest son's house, she was using her cell phone. Molly jumped on her and knocked the cell phone from her hand and then proceeded to eat it. She tried to push Molly away and Molly lunged at the pretty dangling thing that hung from her ear and pulled it out. That was a well behaved day in the life of Molly. Her nickname was "devil dog". I always considered her to be of her father the devil himself. On those occasions when my youngest son would come to visit and brought her with him to our house, much, Much, MUCH against my wishes, she tore into anything she could find. (In his defense the dog had to come along with them to our house or there would have been nothing left of their house if she had stayed home alone.) I was at enmity with Molly and she was most definitely not reconciled to me at that point.

Youngest son's fiancée finally made a bold statement, "Me or the dog!" The dog was passed to my daughter's boyfriend and the misbehavior problems only worsened. More than that, the dog was banned from my house. This is as in "Depart from me into everlasting darkness. I know you not." No, the dog that I love; the dog that I dote on; the dog that everyone hears about all the time; Molly the dog, my dog, was not my dog. That was her condition. The result of that condition was fast approaching, and it wasn't going to be nice.

CHAPTER THREE

"And the dead were judged according to their works, by the things that were written in the books."
Revelation 20:12

Molly had racked up a long list of sins to her account. She was the devil dog and her actions were consistent with her nickname. She had been passed from one master to another with each making the decision that Molly just couldn't stay there anymore. Much could be said, and will be said at another time in her justification, but I recall with great clarity that I was one of her harshest critics and easily noted her many failures. She was not my dog and I was very glad to have her no longer in my home.

Then came "the call". This is one of those defining moments that make a big difference in our lives. It is not on the scale of where were you when the terrorists struck the Twin Towers. No, it is however much more of a defining moment than "what did we have for dinner last night". It is not on the scale of how my mind reeled at the birth of our first child. The incomprehensibility of that new life in my care for the next 18 years or beyond was suddenly overwhelming. I did, though, feel something akin to that the morning after "the call" came.

I was quietly resting in my recliner, reading a book and

halfway watching something on TV when the phone rang. The caller ID said it was our daughter's cell phone so I answered it. (Yes, I do screen phone calls after 9 o'clock and ignore the ones I don't think are important.) "Daddy, (actually she never calls me Daddy anymore, but that is still what I hear) Josh's mom is going to put Molly to sleep tomorrow morning. She nipped at his little brother and she said that was the last straw!"

The woman had been long suffering to the max if truth be told. What the dog hadn't destroyed or damaged in her home would make the short list of what she had left. While normally not aggressive with people, she had seen something in the boy's hand that she wanted and she simply took it. Period! That was reasonably the final straw and putting her to sleep was the final solution. On the level of all honesty I concurred.

But...There is the great decision. But, I intervened. For the sake of my son who seemed, for whatever reason, to have a genuine fondness for the demon with hair, I said the fateful words that changed Molly and me. I said, "I don't want her to do that. (What was I thinking?) Bring Molly here and I will decide what to do with her. No, I don't plan to keep her, but maybe I can find her another home." (Number 6, as I wasn't going to count my home in the equation. She would only be here for a couple of days, after all!!)

What made me change my mind? In the imperfectness of this parable we will call it grace. She was being spared from her justly deserved fate for no other reason than I was going to do it. She hadn't earned any merit in my mind. She hadn't earned any merit in any other adult minds either. Even my son had chosen a girl over her. Granted the girl was wearing an engagement ring, but she still got top billing in his heart over Molly. Even today that lovely girl, who is now his bride, is a tad uncomfortable whenever Molly comes around her. Ah, Molly, you had earned your end and were spared from it by grace alone.

That really is the gist of the matter. Her behavior had earned her rejection after rejection and finally it had earned her the final condemnation. "The wages of sin is death," is a fact known to every believer. Molly was living proof. The books were opened and the facts lay bare. Molly's deeds were recorded in the memory of everyone she encountered. Our minds are imperfect receptacles and God's is perfect. His records are just and true. Our sins have rightly earned full condemnation, but God is gracious to whom He will be gracious and all of the gratitude of the saints should be poured out to Him for exactly that.

My gracious decision had been made. She could stay with us for a few days and be spared the death penalty. My grace surely isn't as great as God's. He doesn't take us in on a trial run. He isn't a holding tank until more suitable accommodations can be found. Praise God for that!! So the parable falls off here a little bit. OK, it falls off a lot.

God's grace is just that, grace. It is completely unmerited. I was moved a little by the thought of what my son would say if I didn't intervene. God's wonderful Son is part of our grace package, to be sure, but God isn't really worried about what His Son will say. They have the same mind, a mind of grace.

We are worthy of full condemnation because we are born in sin, practice sin, love darkness and in general are far worse than we think we are. We deceive ourselves about our inherent goodness when God's Word says we have no inherent goodness. Romans chapter 3 lays out the case strongly against us with words we wouldn't use to describe ourselves: "unrighteous, without understanding, unprofitable, not one doing good, deceitful, poisonous asps, ignorant of the way of peace."

Wow! We don't get up in the morning and look in the mirror and use those words about ourselves, but prior to being saved, to becoming His child, that is exactly the words that God uses to describe us. Not only are we not His child, it is the fact that we don't even care to be His child, to act like His child, to want

His things, thoughts and ways that really defines who we are in the flesh. We are servants of the prince of darkness and slaves to the desires of our fleshly nature. That is who we are in the honesty of the mirror of God's Word which is the only true mirror. While we prefer the mirror of the wicked queen in Sleeping Beauty, it didn't do her any great stead in the end either.

As a consequence of who we are we are justly condemned to be separated from God forever. His holy nature is repulsed at our depravity. Although this is certainly not a popular thought in the last 50 years of theological discussion, it is the truth that the early church, the Reformation church and the mission sending church of the last 200 years preached and taught. Isaiah declared it to the children of Israel, "But your iniquities have separated you from your God; and your sins have hidden His face from you." 59:2

When the children of Israel were punished with the whip of Babylonian conquest and oppression, they had been warned and reaped what they sowed. At the judgment seat of God it will be no different. Mankind will earn their wages. Anything other than earning our wages is the sole benefit of the grace of God.

While we were His enemies and earning the wages of destruction, He was sending His own Holy Son to the cross to die for us. Then in grace He decreed that we could be saved by the blood of His own Son and brought into His family and His home. Then in a further act of grace He interrupted our own selfish ways with the conviction of His Holy Spirit so that we would think of Him instead of ourselves, His goals for us instead of our own and make us aware of His righteousness and our unrighteousness. His grace did it all, planned it all and intervened when we were indifferent to Him. That is His grace.

My grace for Molly wasn't of such stuff as all that. But it does illustrate the point that by grace Molly was saved. As imperfect as my grace was; as limited in scope as it began; with as little love as was part of it, it still saved her from death. How much greater then is God's grace which accomplished our salvation? How much greater God's grace that prompted love enough to crucify His own Son for us? How much greater God's grace that designed from the start to not only spares us from death but to give us His home as our permanent address? The Heidelberg catechism says that such tremendous deliverance as the cross from such great misery as sin and condemnation requires from us a life of singular gratitude.

We need to fly to God in faith. We need to leap into the lap of the Abba (daddy) Father and smother Him with all of our love. We need to make for Him the trinkets of our adoration and display them for all to see. We need to brag about Him to all of our friends. "My Dad's better than your dad." After all, it is true. "My Dad's stronger than your dad." True. "My Dad's smarter than your dad." True again. But the greatest thing that we can say is, "I want to be just like Dad." The greatest thing we can do is practice that statement daily.

Molly can't talk. She can't say any of those wonderful things about me to the other dogs on the block. She can't want to be like me. She is a dog and will always want to be a dog. But she can love me to the extent that dogs love.

When my daughter and her boyfriend brought Molly to the house about 30 minutes after that fateful phone call, Molly did something remarkable to the extent of biblical proportions. She ran into our house and, instead of looking for something to destroy, she ran straight to me. She had never done this before. I was still sitting in my recliner with my book. She didn't hesitate. She made a flying leap straight up into my lap and lay down. She started licking me on the arms and hands and then nuzzled up to my neck and kept it up. Her response to grace was appropriate. Ours should be too.

CHAPTER FOUR

"Come unto Me, and I will give you rest."
Matt. 11: 28

Molly was in our home, or more specifically, in my lap. Suddenly I had a change in plans. That isn't how God's grace works. He planned it from the beginning. No, my imperfect grace mutated at that point. Why not keep this beast and have her become my dog? That was an irrational thought, not God like at all. But it was my thought.

There was a major roadblock to this new goal. My beloved bride was clearly of the opinion that I had been myself until 5 minutes ago. She had no favorable opinions of Molly based on sound grounds. No, she didn't want her to be put to sleep and had agreed to let her stay in our house for a "few" days until better accommodations could be found. That much had been discussed since "the call" had come.

But there were to be major restrictions even on such limited acceptance. She would not have free run of the house or we wouldn't have a house left. Her time limit was one week with a shorter stay preferred. There were others, but since they never came to pass, well, I have forgotten them. Needless to say, the bottom line was still that she was not and would not become our dog.

This was not an easy subject to broach, nor did the discussion go all that well. My beloved bride is a very calm person. She can say "no" very calmly. She can also calmly say "no" repeatedly. She had had experience in the pet department. Our oldest daughter had wanted a dog when she was in the 8th grade. We had two cats at the time and to "prove" herself worthy of having a dog she had to take care of the cats without help for one month. While we were sure that would last one day, she actually made it through the whole month and got her dog. In retrospect we should have had her take care of the cats for 2 months or even a year. One month is about how long she took care of her new dog. Then it became the family dog and "mater" mostly took care of it. That was experience one of many that would follow.

That was 17 years ago and those pets have all returned to their earthly homes. Two other cats have joined the clan since then under similar circumstances and with similar results. You can see that my bride is a most patient and loving spouse and parent. She was also experienced. "Who will walk the dog?" Boldly I asserted that I would. "Who will clean up after the dog?" Bold assertion again. "Who will feed and water the dog?" Further bold assertion. "Right!!!?" she said with a certain tinge of sarcasm. Then she asked them all again and again. Each time I boldly said, "I will."

"OK, but if you don't, she's gone," she calmly said with a smile. A rather crooked smile actually.

And so Molly became my dog. MY DOG! She was adopted by me. Being adopted by me meant that I had certain responsibilities. Most of them had been laid out in our discussion which has been abbreviated for space. Bottom line - I had a dog. Molly was my dog, my adopted dog, and my responsibility.

Once again the parable is weak because I am weak. God is great. He is never caught by surprise. He doesn't make up plans as He goes along. He planned things out before the foundation of the earth. In Isaiah 46:10-11 He says, "My counsel shall stand, and I will do my pleasure…indeed I have spoken it; I will bring it to pass. I have purposed it; I will also do it." Such a God can be trusted with our whole being. He who knows the end from the beginning, who planned the end from the beginning, can certainly take care of me.

That is exactly the point, of course, He can and will take care of me. Why? Because in love He adopted me to be His very own. I became His child by the act of His grace, the purchase of His redemption price and the love of His great heart. Romans 8:15-17 says, "For you did not receive the spirit of bondage again to fear, but you received the Spirit of adoption by whom we cry out, 'Abba, Father'. The Spirit Himself bears witness with our spirit that we are children of God, and if children, then heirs." God planned to adopt me, to call me His child and to give me an inheritance incomprehensible. Molly has been adopted by me and that means a lot of things.

First, she has a new last name. When the vet sends his reminders of her necessary care, they are sent to Molly Craig. She is called by my name. I am reminded of that great climactic moment in the original *Miracle on 34th Street* movie. The lawyer brings in one letter and places it on the judge's bench that is addressed to Santa Claus care of the court house. He reads the official designation of postal codes that requires all mail to be properly addressed and delivered to the appropriate person. The judge is dubious about only one letter so the lawyer has the court clerks bring in all the mail to Santa Claus that the post office has sent to the court house. Case closed. Kris Kringle is the real Santa Claus because the United States Post Office said so. Well, the United States Post Office delivers mail to Molly Craig at my house. Case closed. Acts 11:26 says that believers were first called Christians at Antioch. They had been given a new last name by the community.

Second she has a new nickname. Her moniker of "devil dog" will no longer do. She is Molly Craig and David Craig is no longer a child of the devil and neither is she. Now I call her "Baby". When we go for a walk, "Come here, Baby." When I want her to sit in my lap, "Come here, Baby." More than a few members of my family think that I have reached senility, but I love that term of endearment and use it exclusively for Molly. God calls us His "beloved". John affectionately called the believers "little children." These are terms of endearment that enrich our relationship with our Father. Our relationship with God is not just a theological truth; it is an emotional and relational position. By the Spirit we call Him, Daddy, Father.

Third, Molly has a new owner. Some people hate the idea of ownership, but God employs the concept, why shouldn't we? In I Corinthians 6:19-20 God says, "Or do you not know that your body is the temple of the Holy Spirit who is in you, whom you have from God, **and that you are not your own? For you have been bought with a price**." We are not our own and we never were. We were slaves to sin, servants of the flesh and children of the devil. Christ redeemed us which means that He bought us. He bought us to free us from sin and death, but He didn't buy us to set us free to do our own thing. Our own thing was sin and death. No, He bought us to glorify God the Triune God.

Molly has a new owner and that owner is me. I am God's child and called to live a life of righteousness before Him. Proverbs 12:10 says, "Good people take care of their animals." (GNT) Molly has an owner that takes care of her. Her welfare is a real concern of mine. The second half of Proverbs 12:10 says, "But wicked people are cruel to theirs."

The neighborhood in which I live has a problem with dog fighting. I stopped the man across the street one night when he was training his dog how to fight by having it kill a small cat. After that incident I began to notice in the paper how many dog crimes were being committed in our city. Michael Vick was arrested only a month after I intervened with the man across the street. Not every dog has a good owner.

Satan, our former owner was not a good master. Jesus says of Him, "The thief does not come except to steal, and to kill, and to destroy." John 10:10. Satan offers the pleasures of sin for a season, but the season comes to a quick end. He is a murderer and a liar. He has no care for his own but only desires their destruction.

God is a good owner. In Romans 8:32 Paul says of God, "He who did not spare His own Son, but delivered Him up for us all, how shall He not with Him also freely give us all good things." What a tremendous view of God. His care for us did not stop at the cross for our salvation. He has adopted us. He has made us His own children. He did not spare His Son for our salvation and He will not spare the riches of His glory for our care. Ownership isn't such a bad thing at all if we just have the right owner.

I want to make sure that this is true for Molly. I am her owner and I have been charged by God in His Word to do the job well. Molly came to me at great expense. My beloved bride drove a hard bargain that night. Now it is my responsibility to live up to the standards of a good owner and to finish all that I promised to do.

This is also the promise of God in Philippians 1:6. "He who has begun a good work in you will complete it." God didn't adopt us to abandon us. He adopted us with a plan and purpose that are all for His glory. Doing shoddy work with His children is not for His glory. Satan abandons his own at every opportunity. God keeps His own. His adoption is blessed. Satan required a great price and Christ paid it.

God gave me a new name, a new nickname and new owner. I have done the same for Molly. Coming under His ownership began for me an exciting new life. Coming into my home began a new and different life for me and Molly – **My Dog**.

CHAPTER FIVE

"Old things have passed away, behold all things are become new."
II Corinthians 5:17

It's 6:35 in the morning, and I am definitely not a morning person (but I have said that already) and my fogged mind is clearing. That **IS** *my dog* that is whining. To reinforce that reality, my beloved bride, who is a morning person and happily up and about by this time, comes in to remind me that *"your dog"* is whining. Ah, marital bliss.

Molly came to us with a large kennel in which she had spent the night. It was clear she didn't want to spend the day in it as well. Now, I am opposed to kennels – not as a safe place or a den of retreat – but as a holding cage or restraint mechanism for a dog. Molly had been kenneled 18 or more hours every day for at least the past seven months of her short life.

Her previous owners had asserted that she needed a cage because she was "devil dog" and couldn't be trusted to run free. I had seen her run free the few times she was out of her kennel and knew that they had a point. On the previous night I had been informed by my wife, my beloved bride of 30 plus years, that Molly would still be in the kennel at our house. She was of the inclination that she wanted to find a house to wake up to in the morning.

Isn't it wonderful! There is a parable here. There are many, actually, that we can blend into one.

In Mark 5 Jesus met the "Mad Man of the Gadarenes". This truly was the "devil man". The Bible records that he was possessed of a legion of demons. His behavior was a mirror of Molly's behavior. He ran around tearing things up, resisting all restraint, terrifying the neighborhood and generally being the guy you don't want your daughter to date.

Then he met Jesus. That is the key to all of life. We must meet Jesus. If we don't meet Jesus we will stay in the condition of turmoil that this man was in. Oh, friends, don't deny the turmoil of mankind. People are madly rushing from this fad to that fad, from this TV shrink to the next TV shrink. Self help books are best sellers. People aren't happy with their looks, their incomes, their mates, their employers, their present or their future. They plod through life with every outward appearance of "normalcy", while being seething cauldrons of discontent. The search is on for the next diet, beauty aid, quick fix psychological gimmick, retire early scheme and escape from the mundane opportunity that comes along.

Sadly the church isn't much better. Every day every pastor gets a mailbox full of the newest gimmicks to make "your church better". Christians run from this seminar to that seminar without ever processing the content and seldom even examining its biblical integrity. Churches, run by the people in them, reel from one new program to the next always seeking the perfect fix to the church life's need.

It is time for everyone to stop and meet Jesus. He is found in the Book. We used to say that, "You can find me in the book". Jesus is found in the Book. THE BOOK! In all of our programs, seminars and gimmicks we so often forget to look in the Book. As Sally, a dear saint in my congregation said, "Why don't we stop looking for all the answers in all these other places (our church magazines, books of order, synod meetings) and just look in the Book. Way to go Sally.

When we look in the book we will find Jesus. Jesus will change us. Read on in Mark 5 to verse 15, "Then they came to Jesus, and saw the one who *had been* demon possessed and had the legion, sitting and clothed and in his right mind. And they were afraid". Want to witness successfully to the neighbors? Calm down. Slow down and sit at the feet of Jesus. Feast on His words and be clothed in His righteousness. People will take notice. But, if we run around like they do, always seeking and never seeming to find the answers, they will not fear God or respect our witness.

The Mad Man came to Jesus and what happened? He stopped tearing things up and sat down. He wasn't "mad" anymore. Satan had been a poor master. Satan had left him confused, searching and empty. Jesus gave him peace. What the lost need is to meet Jesus the Savior. What the saved need is to meet Jesus the Lord. Then we all need to sit at His feet and listen and learn and enjoy the peace that passes understanding.

It was time to let Molly out of her cage. She had been restrained long enough by man's means. It hadn't seemed to work too well. She needed to come out of that kennel to her new master. She needed to sit and trust him.

There was something else that was also greatly needed. People had to learn to trust Molly. Too often that is the hardest part. People come to Christ. We know them. We know their past failures. We sit and watch and wait for those failures to erupt again. We wait to see if they are "true" Christians.

What would be far more helpful is if we undertook to disciple them to live like "true" Christians. Many people were raised in the church. They attended Sunday school from the cradle roll onwards. At age four or five they began to sit in "big" church with Mom and Dad. These people say, "But, no one ever came along side and discipled me." Oh? A host of caring people could reasonably disagree.

The first thing that happened to the "Mad Man" was that he sat at Jesus' feet. That is where the Disciples sat. He sat with them. He didn't sit outside the circle. He sat with them. There is no record that all the Disciples sat on one side of Jesus just waiting for the demon to start acting up again. If we say, "But they knew that Jesus had cast it out", aren't we forgetting that He is still in the "casting out" business. If the past of this man could be past, then the past of any man can be past.

As part of our morning worship service each and every Sunday, we pray together the Lord's Prayer. In those beautiful phrases that Jesus taught His own disciples we read this clear line, "forgive us our debts (trespasses for some of our dear brethren) as we forgive our debtors".

I am not so naïve as to not know that some of the congregation can repeat this by memory while sending a text message. For some, in other words, it is a ritual without meaning. It is a canned prayer that can be said without giving a moment's thought to the very Holy God to whom we are supposedly addressing it. (Personally, while I love this prayer and the weekly communal praying of it, I find it much more meaningful as a private meditation, to let the richness of each phrase really speak to me as I speak it to God.)

That thought being put aside, the point is that we are to be forgiving. In forgiving we can start by forgetting. We can accept that "if any man be in Christ He is a new creature." The Bible calls for us to examine the lives of deacons and elders (or pastors) before we elevate them to those offices. Paul tells the Corinthians to note those who are walking and living in Christ and to follow them. There is plenty of room in Scripture for examination of new believers before making them a teacher or leader. There is no room in Scripture for doubting the sincerity of someone's confession simply because we know their past. There is ample room for encouragement, then exhortation and then even discipline, if required, when anyone in the church falls into sin. There is no room for the expectation that old sins will rear their heads. There is no forgiveness in that act. There is no pattern following of Christ, the Disciples or Paul. Paul was rarely in one place long enough to "prove" the "true" Christianity of his converts. We need to present the Word, let the Spirit convict, receive the brethren who respond and welcome them as members into our churches. We need to train, equip and disciple them as members. We need to prove those who are seeking to lead and never advance anyone who isn't seeking to lead to a position of leadership.

To do this we must "let them out of their cage". Their past is past. The restraints of the flesh had failed because they were of far weaker stuff than the restraint of the Spirit of God. The world could not tame what Christ could conquer with a word, a glance, a touch. Christ had opened the cage and let the man out. The Disciples took him into the circle at the feet of Jesus. He was no longer the "devil's man"; now he was "God's man" and the cage of restraint and isolation was no longer necessary.

When my charming daughter-in-law comes to visit, the one whose earring Molly had torn out while also eating her cell phone, she lets Molly sit next to her on the couch. Molly had inflicted real pain upon her. But that is past. Molly now just wants to sit in her lap and give her a licking bath. Kayla has made great strides in accepting the new Molly. We must all do the same for Christ's sake.

Molly was now my dog. I hated the cage as much as she did. The more she had been restrained by man's means, the crazier she had become. Something had to change, and the first thing to do was to open the kennel door.

CHAPTER SIX

"And Enoch walked with God; and he was not, for
God took him."
Genesis 5:24

There is something particularly refreshing about a good walk with a good friend. Indeed there are few activities that I enjoy more than a good walk. It relaxes the body, stimulates the senses and strengthens the heart. These are all things that we need both physically and spiritually.

Jesus was a peripatetic preacher. He taught as he walked. Sure, He stopped by the seaside and sat on the mountain, but there was a lot of time with the disciples when they were just walking along the road. The Gospels record some of those walking discussions, and John tells us that if everything that Jesus said and did were written down it would fill the world with books. That just wouldn't happen if He were silent on all those long walking trips they took.

Moses gives us the command to teach our children about God while we walk by the way. Children like motion. They like to walk and run outside. They were not made for couches or to be plopped inertly in front of a TV. Their bodies want to move. Their little feet were made for walking, and Moses said to teach them about God as they walked by the way.

Enoch walked with God. Did you ever think how cool that would have been? Something about the birth of his son Methuselah stirred Enoch to begin a walk with God. Genesis says that he walked with God after the birth of his son and that he walked with God for 300 years. What did they talk about as they went on walks with each other for 300 years? Perhaps it is a figurative use of the word, but I like to think of walking out along the road with God. What a fantastic picture that is! And then one day instead of sending Enoch back to his own house, God just took him home with Him. Beautiful!

Are we adrift at this point from our topic? No. When I let Molly out of her kennel that first morning, we went for a walk. What she needed was a walk. She is not a lap dog, though she does love to sit on my lap. She is a working/hunting breed. She needs exercise. Ninety per cent of all her behavior problems were related to not getting enough exercise. So we went for a walk. We went a mile and that formulated a pattern that has been followed ever since. Three times a day she gets taken for a one mile walk, each time along a different route.

It is good for her to walk. It is good for her to walk with direction and control. We live in a city. No direction or control would mean squished dog or some other disaster. One night she got loose and one neighbor threatened to shoot her. Since the police were constantly keeping that house under surveillance to catch the occupants in some illegal activity, I believed their threat. Dangers lurk everywhere. There was the other neighbor who was training his dog to fight. Dogs Molly's size make good practice fodder.

Getting run over, being shot or mauled as training bait are some of the bigger dangers for uncontrolled dogs. Smaller dangers lurk even in nicer neighborhoods and smaller towns. Chicken bones in garbage cans, rat poison in small sheds and the list goes on. The world of humans is not a really safe place to be for an unreasoning beast. She needs a collar on her neck and a lead on her collar. Mostly she needs a loving hand at the end of the lead.

Enoch walked with God. The Disciples walked with Christ. Little children walk with their parents. Timothy walked with Paul. The loving hand at the end of the lead is always there. One who knows and cares is walking with one that needs to know. This is discipleship at its purest form.

When Paul wants to give living tips for the Christian life, he uses the word walk repeatedly. In each of his general epistles, to churches not individuals, he uses the theme of how to walk or how not to walk. Of course these are all figurative uses of the term, but they do illustrate the point.

Our life is a walk. On this walk we have the constant presence of the Savior who promised to never leave or forsake us. The Spirit of promise who has sealed us unto the day of redemption (Eph. 1:13-14) is ever present with us. We cannot escape the presence or watch care of God. He is the loving hand at the end of our lead. He is the one who wants to disciple us to grow in Him.

God's hand is on the lead and He desires to take us for a walk, the walk of life. For us to really enjoy this walk with God we need to want to take a walk with Him as well. We need to be eager to have the lead attached to our collar and to walk with Him. In Amos 3:3 it reads, "Can two walk together, unless they are agreed?" He has called us to be His child; He has collared us with His grace; He has engraved on that collar "joint heir with Christ", and now He wants to take us for a walk.

He wants to spend time with us. We are precious to Him. He gave His very own Son to die for our sins. How precious are we? Just look at the cross! And now he wants to have us walk along side of Him every day. He wants us to revel in His presence and rejoice in His ownership.

So we need to be thinking, "I sure do look forward to my walk with God today. I think this is a great idea. I want to learn to walk like He wants me to walk." Now we are in agreement with Him about this walking issue and can enjoy it greatly.

C. Austin Miles puts it so beautifully in that poignant hymn "In the Garden". The chorus goes, "And He walks with me, and He talks with me, and He tells me I am His own; and the joy we share as we tarry there none other has ever known."

So we are walking with Him through the garden of life and He has His gentle hand on the lead. The lead is there for our instruction and our protection. We don't know the way He wants to take and the world won't help us find it. The lead is our friend, not our enemy or an abuse of our being. The lead records for us His will and since we acknowledge that He is our God, knowing His will is very important. It is what we are in agreement upon that we need. He knows we need it and we agree.

His lead for us is found in His Word. In Psalm 32:8 God says, "I will instruct you and teach you in the way you should go." Paul tells Timothy in II Timothy 3:16, "All Scripture is given by inspiration of God, and is profitable for doctrine, for reproof, for correction and for instruction in righteousness."

God walks with us each day. He guides us each day. That walk and that guidance come through the Holy Scriptures. If we want to enjoy our time with Him, we need to let Him lead, to listen to His direction. This calls upon us to walk daily in the Word. As a pastor I am intensely concerned that my people walk daily in the Word. While intentions are good, a plan is better. I don't intend to walk Molly sometime; I plan to walk Molly every day after breakfast, lunch and supper. I don't just want people to intend to read their Bible sometime; I put in the bulletin each Sunday a simple devotional reading guide for that week. They have a planned reading schedule (and of course, since I have the best congregation in the world, they all use it faithfully each day.)

God walked with Enoch. Christ walked with His disciples. God wants us to have a good walk with Him. Christ wants us to see Him as our very own peripatetic teacher. He is not just the Christ of long ago. He is the Christ who is alive and desiring the same intimate walk with us as He had with the twelve in Galilee. He needed to prepare and equip them for life, life in a world contrary to His ways, His thoughts, His ideas, His love, His purpose.

Life is dangerous, not just for dogs, but for us as well. This world is not a friend of God. They did not receive His Son with open arms. Isaac Watts asks the question "Is this vile world a friend of grace to bring me home to God?" (Hymn – "Am I a Soldier of the Cross?) The answer is a resounding NO!

While a garden is the ideal picture of our walk with Christ, the reality is more like a wilderness. God walked with the children of Israel in the wilderness for 40 year. He never left them even in their grossest times of disobedience. He fed them the manna, gave them water to drink from the rock, sheltered them under the coolness of the cloud by day and protected them by the fire at night. He directed them in the way that they should go when they had no clue where they were going. In the hostile environment of the great desert He walked with them. The history of the Exodus records that they would have had a better time, enjoyed the experience much more and gained a great deal of benefit if they had just wanted to walk with Him as well. They ignored the lead and paid the price. Let us walk joyously in agreement with our Master. Let us do it every day to our benefit, to the rapture of our souls as we discover more of His great love for us.

CHAPTER SEVEN

"Thy Word is a light unto my path."
Psalm 119:105

The prophet Amos makes a profound statement, "Can two walk together, unless they are agreed?" (3:3) What wisdom of God is encapsulated in those eight short words. To go on a walk there should be basic agreement on the destination, the path and the pace. Without those conditions a walk can be torture for one or all of the participants.

That might be the proper description for that first walk with Molly. In Ephesians 4:17 Paul admonishes the believers to "no longer walk" like you did before you were saved. Before you were God's child, he tells them, you walked in futility, ignorance, blindness, darkness and all the corrupt desires of the flesh. Now, he says, you are God's children, and that is not how God's children are to walk.

Molly was now my dog. She was no longer "devil dog". I love to walk. It may be my favorite past time. My bride and I go on hiking vacations. We like to go to places where there are lakes to walk around, hills to climb, and historic streets to stroll through. Before setting out on these long walks we do set down the expectations for the day. "We will get in eight miles this morning and then take a break. After lunch we will hit this other five mile stretch that we want to see." We have now settled on the destination, the path and the pace. That is how we walk.

That is not how we walked that first morning with Molly. (Yes, we. My bride was up and wanted to see this show – me walking "devil dog" – in person.) If she had paid money for the experience she would have had her money's worth. Molly had a destination in mind – wherever she wanted to go. She had a pace in mind – either stop and sniff or tear as fast as possible after a squirrel. Her path was entirely dictated to her by her destination and her pace. We had some work to do.

When we come to Christ we have no sense of spiritual direction. We have been used to going our own way and doing our own thing. Our own thing could have been well disciplined or very haphazard. Our own way could have been that of restrained morality or unrestrained immorality. Our own way could have been either religious or irreligious. It matters not whether in the sight of man it was good or bad, right or wrong, honorable or dishonorable. It was not God's way. It was ours.

Many people prefer to think that their way wasn't "that bad". They are glad that their personal testimony doesn't include all those issues that others stand and testify about. They were not abusers of drugs, alcohol, sex, pornography, spouses, gambling or assorted other "major sins" that other people have committed. That our outward life was seemingly acceptable to man does not mean that it was acceptable to God. If it were, then why did we need to get saved?

That means that we enter into this new relationship with God with a profound need to learn His system. We need to know His way. We need to understand His directions. Isaiah 55:8 sums it up clearly when God says, "For My thoughts are not your thoughts, nor are your ways My ways." Paul says that our ways were darkness, futility, etc. No matter how they appeared to man; they appeared to God as not His ways. There is, therefore, a lot of work to be done on getting this walking thing straight.

Molly and I had work to do. We and God have work to do. What is the first step in the process? Since we are walking together we need to have a plan. Since Molly is a dog, she doesn't have a plan. That means that I have to have a plan. Since we don't have a clue about God's thoughts, if we are going to walk joyfully with Him, then we need to let Him have the plan.

We are no more entitled to co-opt God and say, "Let's plan this together" than Molly could say to me, "Let's plan this together." We are not God's equal. We are His purchased possession. Molly is not my equal. PETA may disagree, but in reality she is my dog. I plan the trips. I set the agenda. I set the pace. We are God's possession. He plans the trip. He sets the agenda. He sets the pace. Someone in this relationship must be the Master and the other the one with the Master – the servant of the Master or the master's dog.

Who is going to lead in our lives is the single most important decision that we can make minute by minute, hour by hour and day by day. We want to sniff. God wants to walk. We want to chase squirrels. God wants to walk. We want to chase across the yard after a cat. God wants to stay on the narrow way (the sidewalk.) We don't care whose lawn we soil. God does. Are we the hand holding the lead, or are we the one being led?

This is not a final decision that we make today and keep forever. Read the Gospels and see how many times that just when you think the Disciples were "getting it", they really weren't. The next verse reveals the fact that there was a long way to go. Paul, in Romans 7, laments that he can't get it straight. He wants to obey God, but then he doesn't obey God.

Molly looks at me so expectantly each day before our walks. She is excited and with many slobbery kisses and wags of her tail she promises that today is the day that we will get it right. I am a gullible dog owner. I pet her head and tell her what a good girl she is and we set off. I am rejoicing at how well things are going; and then she sees the first squirrel of the day. Good intentions, slobbery kisses, wagging tail and big brown eyed promises are forgotten.

That is really how it is with us and God. We don't get up and tell God that we plan to sin today at 7:30, 7:45, 7:51, 8:02 and so on. We pray and with sincere devotion we ask Him to guide our steps, keep our thoughts and give us His purpose. We are set for the day, or not! A child, pick any one of them (we had six), spills orange juice all over themself with just one minute before the bus will arrive. That child that we hoped for, prayed for and prayed through many an infant/toddler illness is now not the source of our sincere love and adoration. We will be late for work. A *million* unpleasant scenarios erupt in our mind from this one incident. Our thoughts are no longer godly nor God like. It is only 7:30 and His thoughts are no longer our thoughts. Ah! Life! It is time to recheck the hand on the lead.

This walking stuff is difficult. Children are not born walking. (Praise the Lord for that!) Parents have some semblance of control for a while. Then the crawling begins. How many times have the babies crawled where we didn't want them to crawl? Eventually they pulled themselves up on something and we oohed and aahed at their wonderful progress. Then they took their first step and we called the grandparents to share the momentous occasion. Then they walked where we didn't want them to go.

So, we put up baby gates. Our three year old grandson reaches across, unhooks the tension bar, walks through and then reattaches the tension bar. It is a wonderfully successful tool for keeping him where we want him to be. Their thoughts are not our thoughts. The laws of the "god of the house" (mommy or daddy) are of no concern to them. They have a sinful self-will, and they will exercise it. Yes, that beautiful child is a sinner and God says of him, "the imagination of a man's heart is evil from his youth". (Gen. 8:21) The Hebrew here denotes a young and dependent child.

Walking starts out going the wrong way. We crawled the

wrong way; we walk the wrong way. Our ways are simply not God's ways. We can't stay walking that way and please God with our lives any more than the little child can go wherever he wants and please Mommy. Someone has to be in charge. Someone has to know the boundaries and the destination. Someone who is wiser and greater and loving must lead the way. It is not an act of brutality or dominance for the sake of power that requires someone to have control. It is the hand of love, of care, of compassionate wisdom that must lead. Their hand must be on the lead or there will be disaster.

That first morning with Molly was a scene you can only imagine. It brought to my mind how truly thankful I am that I am not God. In Mark 4 Jesus tells His disciples that they are going to go across the lake. He didn't say they might make it to the other side. He said, "Let us cross over to the other side". (v. 35) Along the way a terrible storm came up. The Disciples lost all faith in their trip and their Master. They accused Him of being indifferent and uncaring. He didn't abandon them and walk the rest of the way by Himself. No, He rebuked the storm and took His disciples across.

We had a very stormy first walk. I wondered greatly if I really wanted to be "this" dog's owner or not. I knew that I had the full support of my bride if I chose the "or not". Remember, she was getting her money's worth. I was frankly very tempted to make our home just stop number 6 on a further odyssey of failure for Molly. But then I thought of God. What would God do? What would God think? Would the God who promised to NEVER leave me cast me aside for my sin? He said He wouldn't. He said that we would go across. I would just have to teach Molly how to walk. She was, after all, my dog. And, she still is.

CHAPTER EIGHT

"As each of you has received a gift, minister it to one another."
I Peter 4:10

The believer has an edge over Molly. When we come to Christ He gives us His Holy Spirit who dwells within us. He teaches us of Christ. He convicts us of sin. He is the Holy Spirit and guides us to live a holy life. That is our advantage. Sadly many believers don't avail themselves of this great gift. They think His conviction is indigestion. They find no time daily to be taught of Him in the Word of God. They would choose the pleasures of the world's approval over a holy life. Nevertheless, He does indwell the believer and make possible walking the right walk the right way a whole lot easier than if everything must be an external situation only.

For Molly there is no Holy Spirit within her to help her obey. There is training, training, training. There is practice, practice, practice. There is repetition, repetition and repetition. While every believer needs all three of these elements to grow and walk correctly with God, the Holy Spirit is within them to help them grasp the matters at hand and to grow successfully for the glory of God. Molly lacks internal help.

Here Molly is rather like the lost person who wants to appear religious. The whole inner nature of sin is fighting against the law of God. The desire to obey the law is present only to the extent that there is some gain to be had from the external appearance of godliness. This desire does not flow from the Spirit of God and does not curb the inner desire to sin, only the external evidence of sin. It is tough to walk against our nature without the help of God's Spirit within us.

It reminds me of a story I read in the paper. A police dog was killed in the line of duty. After having successfully identified drugs in the hubcap of a car, the dog was rewarded with its ball. Unfortunately, the ball fell from the dog's mouth and rolled into the highway. The dog chased its ball and was struck by a passing car. The dog was doing what dogs do – it was chasing its ball. It was a highly trained dog. It was efficient at doing what it was supposed to do. It had all the outward marks of being the perfectly trained dog, but with no inner sense of reason, it chased the ball into the highway and died.

The lost person trying to walk the Christian walk may appear to have won the fight with the flesh. They haven't. Training, discipline and repetition fail at the decisive hour. That hour may not be until the Day of Judgment, and failure at that point is double death – the death of the body and the eternally judged death of the soul apart from its maker. Sadly for those who try to establish their own righteousness, they miss the true righteousness of God and the hope, peace and eternal life that offers. Paul deals with this issue at length in Romans 2.

While the lost person could abandon their goal of self-righteousness and fall on the grace of God, Molly has no such recourse. Molly has received my grace and lives in my house and now it is my influence, my external guidance that must make her into the good dog that I want her to be. So, let the training begin.

This was going to be a snap, I thought. I checked the phone book for dog obedience schools and found one. That isn't as if I had my choice and found many and chose one, I found ONE. How many choices do we really need – right? So, we called and enrolled Molly.

Now, in all honesty, I had pictured we would find something like the American Kennel Club annual dog show. NOT! It was in the back room of the local pet supply store and the only student was Molly. One on one attention is the goal of a good education. We were going to get that.

A lot of people avoid small churches for exactly the wrong reason. They don't want to stand out. Anonymity is wrong on multiple levels, but a chief one is that it also equates to no accountability. Our faith walk needs accountability. The author of Hebrews challenges us with accountability when he says, "Therefore we also, since we are surrounded with so great a cloud of witnesses, let us lay aside every weight, and the sin which so easily ensnares us, and let us run with endurance the race that is set before us." (12:1) All those witnesses are going to keep us on the straight and narrow. A face in the crowd has no witnesses. We need to be seen. We need to be known.

The church is a body and the health of each part is essential to the health of the whole. Accountability leads to good health. Our local TV station is channel 7. On the 7th day of each month they have a women's health accountability day. The reasoning is that if someone is holding a person accountable they are more likely to take care of necessary issues with their life. The same is true of a smaller congregation. This is also why many larger churches develop small accountability groups. Anonymity is bad. Accountability is good.

Molly was not anonymous. She was the only dog in the class. We either had to get it right, or she would FLUNK! That's right. My children were all honor scholars (truth), but my dog, well, it could FLUNK! My bride was rather of the opinion that that would be the outcome. I was rather of the opinion that Molly would be first in her class.

Here is where my bride really stepped up to the plate with Molly. Training was offered when I was at work. My beloved bride was the one who had to take her and train her. This increased Molly's accountability group to three – me, my bride and the teacher. I wanted to see results when she got home. They wanted to see results when she was at school.

This is good accountability. Our walk with God isn't just for one situation only. We need to be held accountable in every situation of our life. Do you ever read the signs on the back of trucks? I like the ones that say, "How's my driving? If it's not OK call 555-555-5555." That trucker is now accountable to every person on the road. Perhaps all believers should wear a lapel pin that says, "Hi. I'm a Christian. How am I doing?" Maybe every Christian should have a desk plate in their cubicle that reads, "Hi. I'm a born again Christian. How is my Christ-likeness today?"

Instead of giving ourselves over to "good accountability", here are two sad realities. One is that we choose often to worship in anonymity. I know this because people can be surprisingly honest and tell me so. They almost refer to it as "no pressure" Christianity. The second sad reality is that we tell no one that we are a believer in Jesus Christ and can therefore hide our Christianity on a daily basis.

Molly was in a perfect situation. She was accountable to Jacque (my bride) and to the teacher every day at school. She was accountable to me at home. In the ideal setting and outside of the ideal setting, she was accountable to be trained well.

I encountered this strange and unpleasant situation once in my pastoral role. I was visiting with a non-churched person. I was inviting them to come to our church. I did something that I don't often do. I dropped a name. So-and-so goes to our church. You know them don't you? Yes, they knew them. No, they didn't know that they went to our church. Yes, they knew them well. They had known them for years! No, it had never come up. Actually they seemed genuinely surprised that So-and-so went to church at all. Well, So-and-so had been a member of our church for almost forty years. Inside the church walls they were esteemed. Outside the church walls their faith was unknown. I contrast that with another family in church who post on the door of their business that they attend our church and that their business is closed on Sunday and all their customers are invited to come and worship with them and all of us each week.

Believers were not born again by God to hide in the pews or slip unnoticed through life. Likewise they were not born again by God to shine in the pews and slip unnoticed through life. We are born again by God into the body of Christ where we need to have true engagement with our fellow believers that results in a dynamically effective walk with God before the world. Paul says to the Thessalonians, "In every place your faith toward God has gone out, so that we do not need to say anything. For they themselves declare concerning us what manner of entry we had to you, and how you turned to God from idols to serve the living and true God." (1:8-9)

The crucible of our faith is not church, it is the world. We need to be in church as the training school for our faith. We need to be faithful to the preaching of the Word and to the practices of the faith. In that setting we also need to be active in such ways that we are transparent to our real self and therefore accountable to our walk with God. Just showing up will not do that. But we also need to take our faith walk with us every day. Our training is no good if it doesn't work on the street.

That was the real challenge of the training of Molly. Could she walk well in the back of the store with no one else around? Could she walk just as well on the street with multiple distractions? Then the greater question is simply this: "Can we?"

CHAPTER NINE

"For the good that I will to do, I do not do; but the evil that I will not to do, that I practice."
Romans 7:19

Paul makes this remarkable statement. Who is a greater example to us of the Christian life than Paul who says in I Corinthians 11:1, "Be imitators of me." This verse in Romans 7 is not some reflection on his former life; it is a commentary on his everyday life. This is made clear in Romans 7:24 when he adds, "O wretched man that I am." Not that "I was", but that "I am"! He needed an everyday deliverer from the bondage of the flesh that still molested him and all the Christian family. What comfort that I am not alone when I fail!

Oh, yes, I fail. You fail. Paul failed. Peter failed, not just before the crucifixion of Christ, but he had to be openly rebuked by Paul for His sin in Galatians 1:11-16. It is not that we should rejoice in failure of others. No! But we can take encouragement that these robust believers had their down moments. It wasn't what they wanted to practice, but it was what happened to them as men still living in the flesh. Not only can we draw some slight encouragement from this, not an encouragement to sin, but encouragement that others who have experienced a practice of sin when they wanted to practice

41

righteousness didn't give up, but got up and kept on walking for the Lord. So can we!

There is a certain foundation here for training a dog to walk – especially a dog which had been known as the "devil dog". This was not going to be a slam dunk one walk and we're fully trained scenario. No. If I am prepared to admit that I still live like the frustrated Paul who bared his honest soul in Romans 7, then I must harbor some small compassion for others who do the same. In this case, Molly. I would rather that she didn't often fail to walk obediently, but she did.

There were demons that plagued her – metaphorically, of course. Her demons were of the four legged variety that she simply couldn't resist. There was the demon Rottweiler, the demon collie, the demon mutt, the demon cocker spaniel, the demon Grey hound and the list goes on. There were wily "wabbits" (thank you Bugs Bunny) and worst of all the seductive squirrels. It was in her unrestrained and untrained heart to vigorously pursue each and every one of these four footed distractions. I literally had to see a doctor to deal with the damage that Molly did to my back and shoulder muscles and bones.

Molly is as acrobatic with her body as many people are with their tongues. Paul admits that he fell into the flesh and didn't walk by the spirit. Many people try to make excuses instead. They can be very entertaining with their verbal gymnastics to try and wiggle out of straightforward confession and repentance. Molly was entertaining to many people on the street.

She can jump straight up in the air six feet. While in the air she can do as many twists and turns as an Olympic diver. She can hit the ground on her back paws only and pirouette as rapidly as a ballerina. People would stop and stare. Cars would slow down to see the performance. She would go through every contortion possible to get her goal.

Her first goal was to rid herself of the restriction of the collar and leash. She could indeed slip out of it with her many maneuvers. Then she was off and didn't want to come when called. She would run down rabbits, climb trees after squirrels (that is very true) and generally create a cacophony of barking by pestering every dog within six blocks that were penned in their yards. It was Molly versus the world.

It is my desire as Molly's owner to personify human characteristics into her. I really want to personify good characteristics into her. I want to think that she really wanted to be a good dog but that she was simply struggling to get it done. The cry of Molly's heart was, "Who will deliver me from being this wretched dog that I am."

I love my dog. I really do. God loves me. He really does. I often imagine God looking at me and slapping his forehead and saying, "Oi! Why did I choose him." At least that is often how I felt about Molly. God intervenes daily to deliver me from the wretched man that I am and change me into His likeness. I must do the same for Molly.

We had demons to deal with. We had behaviors to control. We had work to do. Mostly, I had work to do. We have the advantage of God's Holy Spirit within us to help us with the work of growing and changing. He has also given us the responsibility to use the minds that He has given us to accomplish this task. Paul writes to the Romans and tells them to "renew their minds" in order to prove the will of God in their lives. (12:1-2) Even in this God gave us a mind to think and the Bible to guide. It is God working in us to perfect His glory. Our job is not to be distracted by the demons, not to break the leash, but to sit and listen and then obey.

What are our demons? For each person they come in a different package. For some it may be the demon Rottweiler of Rum. For the next it might be the Collie of Conformity to the world. For the next it might be the Greyhound of Greed. It might be the Bull Dog of Boastfulness or the Poodle of Pride. It might be the Great Dane of Gossip or the Pekingese of Pornography. We come into our Christian faith with them already intact in our lives. As certainly as the demoniac of the Gadarenes knew that He had a problem, we have been convicted by God of our own sin and come to Him as needy sinners to be saved by His grace.

But coming to Him does not leave behind the track record of indulgence in the demons of the flesh that we have been so used to worshipping. In times past Paul tells the Ephesians, "we also once conducted ourselves in the lusts of our flesh, fulfilling the desires of the flesh and of the mind." (2:3) This calls for the renewing of the mind and the putting off of the flesh. This we can do as we are obedient to the leading of the Spirit of God.

This I had to do for Molly, and she had to learn to follow me. Instead of walking down the sidewalk within hissing distance of dogs clamoring at their fence, we walked in the street. Slowly she learned this way to ignore the dogs that were now thirty or more feet away. She paid attention to me and not to them. Paul tells Timothy in II Timothy 2:22 to "flee youthful lusts." That command is the lead on the collar. That is God directing our steps to walk in the street and not next to the damaging demons that plagued our life before we were saved.

He doesn't say to cozy up to the old ways. He tells us to abandon the old ways. If that means walking down the opposite side of the street from every tavern in town; if that means cancelling the subscriptions to the magazines that make us want to be more like the world; if that means to stop dining in the casino restaurant because it is in the casino, then we need to walk away from youthful lusts, from the past of sin that "so easily ensnares us" (Hebrews 12:1) and then to "run with endurance the race that is before us" (Hebrews 12:1).

God's Word is the lead that guides us just as certainly as the lead on Molly's neck is the one that is to guide her. We can tug and pull on the lead, we can try to break away from it and we can argue and fight – but why? Has not God saved us from the very things that we now seek? Did the Holy Spirit Himself not convict us at the beginning that the way of sin led to the judgment of God? Was there not a Spirit led consent to this truth on our part and a Spirit induced commitment to the Savior who had saved us from the destruction of such things?

God, in His ongoing mercy, calls us daily to walk in newness of life. His mercy is extended for the glory of His grace as Paul tells us in Ephesians 1:6, "to the praise of the glory of His grace." It is to be acted out in our lives that "we who first trusted in Christ might be to the praise of His glory." (Ephesians 1:12)

The lust of the flesh, the demons of the world, the wily "wabbits" of worldly wisdom and the seductive squirrels of sensuality are always present around us each day. We live in the flesh and will live in the flesh until our full redemption is complete in the personal presence of Christ. But, living in the flesh is not to demand of us that we live for the flesh.

Because these dangers to our walk to the "praise of His glory" lurk everywhere, we need to diligently heed the lead of Christ upon the neck of our spiritual walk. Our walk may not be pretty at times. It may come with frustrations as the flesh wins some daily battles. But it should come with the clear conviction that our true desire is to walk led by the Spirit of God, to be more sensitive to our failures, more committed to fleeing the lusts of the flesh and to walking more faithfully and quietly right by the Savior's side "to the praise of His glory." Let the world stand amazed at the new us. I Peter 4:3-5.

CHAPTER TEN

"If we say we have no sin, the truth is not in us."
I John 1:8

Have I ever mentioned yet that I love my dog? I am not scientifically dispassionate about Molly. As a human being, then, I personify human traits into my dog that may not actually exist. They are great for illustrations or the basis of parables, but they are not really part of her canine make-up. Human emotion can override human intellect and create a strange amalgam of ideas. Molly is part of our family and I like to think of her in human terms. My beloved bride prefers to think of her as a dog.

This issue recently became an item for discussion. A "scientific" study was done to test whether dogs actually feel guilt. We have been discussing in the last chapter about becoming more sensitive to God's will and our true condition of rebellion to it. Our walk is going to be based in large part on a better understanding of what our real nature is like in comparison to God's. Few people actually feel as Paul did in his self-condemning comments about his current wretched condition. Along these lines came the study about dogs and guilt. It presented a challenging thought.

Are we dogs? Actually that is more the end of the thought than the beginning, but it could come either place. The "scientific" conclusion of the study was that dogs don't feel guilt. They are care free irrational creatures who only reflect the guilt we project onto them. If we are indifferent to the spilled garbage, the chewed slipper or the muddy paw prints on the couch, they will be too. Only as we notice these things and generate a sense of agitation about them does the dog "feel" guilty. Their drooping head and tail are not because they care at all about what they did. They care because we care what they did and they respond to our negative reaction to the event. Are we dogs?

Does sin bother us because we know it is wrong, or does sin only bother us when we consider the consequences from a holy God? Is the only time that we feel guilty is when we have fouled up to such an extent that we fear actual retribution from a righteous judge, or are we so in tune with the Word and will of God that we are prepared to confess the smallest departures from the path of the "praise of His glory"?

Let us distinguish here two groups of people. The world is not divided into multiple categories. God only gives us two – His own and NOT His own. Apart from Christ we were all once not His own. Through personal faith in the crucified and resurrected Lord Jesus we become His own. Paul states in I Corinthians 15:1-4 this very basic truth, "Moreover, brethren, I declare to you the gospel which I preached to you, which also you received...by which also you are saved...for I delivered to you first of all that which I also received: that Christ died for our sins according to the Scriptures, and that He was buried, and that He rose again the third day according to the Scriptures." They personally, each one, received the Good News, the gospel; they believed it by faith and became a child of God. They became His own.

The rest are simply NOT His own. They may become His own by personal faith the same as those who are His own, but until they do, they are not His own. Paul, in his letter to the Ephesians includes himself in this changing of categories. In chapter 2 verse 3 he says, "Among whom also **_WE_** once conducted ourselves in the lusts of our flesh, fulfilling the desires of the flesh and of the mind." Paul does not stipulate that because someone is not God's own, that they are permanently mired in that state. He only asserts that until they are quickened (made alive) by God (Ephesians 2:1 and 5) and brought by Him to saving faith, that they are not His own as Paul was himself also once not His own.

Now Paul wants to make distinctions between the two categories. In Ephesians 4:17-19 he states, "This I say, therefore, and testify in the Lord, that you should no longer walk as the rest of the Gentiles walk, *(note the following descriptions)* **1.** in the **futility** of their mind, **2.** having their **understanding darkened**, **3.** being **alienated** from the life of God, **4.** because of the **blindness** of their heart, **5.** who, being **past feeling**..." In Romans 1:21 Paul again addresses those who have no faith in Christ as the only Savior of man, "Because, although they knew God, they did not glorify Him as God, nor were thankful, *(note the following descriptions)* **1.** but became **futile** in their thoughts, **2.** and their foolish hearts were **darkened**. Professing to be wise, **3.** they became **fools**." Paul would obviously not be invited back to speak a second Sunday in most modern churches.

Back to the question, are we dogs? (Be honest, you thought I forgot about that question and just went rambling off somewhere.) What Paul is saying about the lost is that they don't care about soiling the sofa, spilling the garbage and chewing the slippers in God's house. They are blind to the will of God. They are darkened from the conviction of the Word of God. They are past feeling about the things of God. Only when the law comes crashing down on them and the righteous Judge holds them before His court do they care at all.

God does not say that these people can't be loyal and loving and kind. He doesn't say that they can't make good neighbors or co-workers. He says that they are indifferent to HIM, past feeling about HIM, foolish in regard to HIM, and since He is the eternal God, this is very bad for them. They are indeed like dogs.

But of us the same thing should not be said. We are not like dogs. We have been changed. We have been born again and made into a new creation. It is now not the external face of God's anger that awakens us. We are His children. We are not dogs. As His children we have His Holy Spirit living within us. We have His Word in front of us and the Holy Spirit teaching it to us.

The new man, as Paul repeatedly calls us, is awake to God, sensitive to God, alert to self, especially the failures of self in the light of the truth of God. The closer we walk in the light of God the more evident those failures of self will appear. When things are far from the light they are obscure and hard to distinguish. As children of God we are called to walk in the light of God. Psalm 119:105 says, "Your word is a lamp to my feet and a light to my path." We need to obediently bring our lives more and more into the light of God. We need the revelation of His light to truly light our path in a dark world that is indifferent or hostile to Him.

As this walk with God becomes more intimate the more honestly we will see ourselves. We will not need our Master walking into the room with a scowl. We will not wait to respond to His overt reaction to our sin. We will know our Master. We will know His will. We will CARE. Paul's cry in Romans 7:24 "Who will deliver me from this body of death?" reveals that inner awareness. He didn't need the Master's external scowl of disapproval. He was imprinted by rebirth with the divine nature (II Peter 1:4) "by which have been given to us exceeding great and precious promises, that through these you may be partakers of the divine nature".

The imprinting of the divine nature, being born of the Spirit of God, places us in the category of those who are His. Now it is God's guidance through the new nature of the new birth that brings us to a closer walk with Him. We know Him because we are a part of Him and He is a part of us. In a miraculous way there is a new DNA code in our body. It is not one detectable by the mechanical means of men's technology. It is revealed in the new life that is within us. It is revealed by the character of what we are becoming. It is revealed by our response to the truth as taught in His Word.

This is not the case with man and dog. I say that Molly is "my dog". She is, but in a purely humanistic and worldly speaking way. I could waste a lot of money by taking some of her blood and some of my blood to the clinic and having them evaluate the DNA to see if she is really "mine" or not. We all know what the results of that test would be. I can anthropomorphize my attitudes and thoughts into her actions, but it is an illegitimate attempt to make her more than what she is. I can't change her into a human. She is a dog.

But, God can change us! That is the really good news! He can take a sinful human, walking in the futility of their mind, the blindness of their heart, and indifferent to the things of God and to God Himself, and He can change that human into His own child. He has done it through the cross of Calvary. He has done it by putting Jesus blood on us and imparting to us through the blood of His own Son His own divine nature.

Paul's plea for deliverance is not guilt unanswered. It is an exclamation of delight in the finished work of God. By God's imparted nature Paul saw Himself as he really was. His guilt was true, not feigned to please an angry Master. His guilt was also not hopeless. He knew that he only knew of his guilt because he was God's own child. His happy conclusion was not hanging his head and slinking off to his corner in reaction to external shame. No. His reaction was to give praise to Christ who had saved him, and so he ends the issue with this proclamation, "I thank God, through Jesus Christ our Lord!"

CHAPTER ELEVEN

"But grow in grace and knowledge of our Lord and
Savior Jesus Christ."
II Peter 3:18

I would like to emphatically state that Molly never has anything to cause her a sense of guilt even if she could have one. I would like to state that, but I can't. No honest parent of a two year old could say that. At some time in my life I read an article that stated that dogs can never, even at their best trained ability and for the smartest breeds, achieve a capacity for understanding and cognition above that of a two year old child. Since Molly is, of course, the best trained dog of the smartest breed, I can therefore expect from her what I can expect from my two year old grandson. He never seems to have a sense of guilt either, but he certainly should.

Molly is a very good dog and she is well trained. She can sit and . . . well, she can sit. Staying put is another proposition altogether. She will go to the door if she has to go to the bathroom. Unless she doesn't, but that really isn't a huge problem as she has options. Someone in the early years of her life before she became my dog trained her to use paper. When she doesn't go to the door she goes to the basement where I have left a small corner area covered with paper for her use. She has a budding vocabulary. She knows sit, walk and outside. Without a movement of any kind on my part she responds appropriately to those three words. Alright, Molly doesn't exactly qualify for being two just yet, but she is a good dog.

This means that Molly has some room for growth. There is a lot of raw potential in her. I know it. I tell it to my *beloved bride* often. Molly is definitely not "that stupid dog" as *some* would assume. No, she definitely will grow more able as time goes on.

We had that certain hope when our six children were toddlers. This can't go on forever we often reassured ourselves. Now we try to pass that reassuring hope along to our children who have children of their own. It is not that while they are in the middle of the fray, so to speak, they believe a word we say. They simply smile and say thank you and are waiting to place us in a home for the senile.

The reality is that the child who throws a fit at the table because they cannot communicate their needs or desires will indeed learn to speak and share in a more appropriate way what they want. I know perfectly well what my children will say at that stage of development. "Oh, I wish they were still young enough to not talk." But if they didn't talk there would be something wrong with them. They are meant to grow and develop and we are meant to help them.

I remember well a problem we had with our fourth child's development. He didn't talk until he was five. He wouldn't open his eyes to look at the eye chart for the eye doctor. He wouldn't respond with so much as a nod of the head to the speech clinician. We knew he could see because he didn't run into things and pointed at what he wanted. As to hearing, well, we didn't know. By age three he displayed multiple signs of autism, but we had him checked by a specialist for that as well and he didn't. His body was strong and healthy, but his behavior was quite unnatural and his speech just wasn't.

We were concerned because he wasn't growing correctly. We

were his parents and he was our concern. Even his older siblings expressed concern about behavior and speech problems he had. They were his siblings and it was their concern as well. Proper growth and development is a genuine concern for all members of the family.

Today son number four is in seminary following in the footsteps of dear old dad. He is the minister to the deaf at his church and is planning on doing church planting work to the deaf community. No, he is not deaf. Once he started to talk he never shut up. It did take four years of speech therapy before we could understand him, but he did grow and develop. There was no serious problem.

Our oldest grandson is a real pistol. In reality that would be a machine gun pistol. He is always going off loud and long. He is, in fact, just like his mother, our oldest child when she was his age. Since he learned to walk she would repeatedly call us in or near tears. She didn't know if either of them would survive his terrible one's, then more terrible two's and then hyper-terrible three's. We assured her that we had survived her. We reminded her that she had grown up to be responsible and successful but that her beginnings had left all that in doubt. Love him, set reasonable boundaries and don't expect twenty year old behavior from while he is still just two we told her. Now he is four and I had a very pleasant lunch with him a few weeks ago. He is growing up.

Whether it is a dog, a child or a grandchild, they don't start out where you want them to end up. We begin at the beginning. We all did and, until Christ comes back, everyone will. The issue isn't where we start. The issue is how we move on from there.

Jesus says that coming to faith in Him is being called born again. (John 3:6-7) This time we are not born by the will of the flesh, mom and dad creating this new human being, but by the will of the Spirit. John says, "Who were born, not of blood, nor of the will of the flesh, nor of the will of man, but of God." (1:13) Paul puts it like this, "Therefore, if anyone is in Christ, he is a new creation; old things have passed away; behold all things have become new." (II Corinthians 5:17)

We start out our life in Christ as a new creation. We are newborns. Peter calls us newborn babes in First Peter 2:2, "As newborn babes, desire the pure milk of the word, that you may grow thereby." We have to get started all over again. Our speech patterns have to be learned. Our walking has to be learned. The rules of life have to be learned. We don't start out where we will end up. We aren't what we should become. There is real growth potential in every one of us.

In life there are periodic checkups. We had two new grandchildren born in the past month. It seems they are always going to the doctor. Why, I asked. There is the first week checkup and then the two week checkup. There might be a one month checkup and a two month checkup. That is a lot of checkups. Then there will be the six month checkup and the nine month checkup and the one year checkup. Since we babysit the older ones while the younger ones have their checkups, we are learning about checkups. There seem a lot more of them than when our children were small.

There will be a whole new set of checkups for the children when they reach school age. There will be exams in math and English and spelling and reading. Are they making progress? There will be annual exams of basic skills. Are they making progress? They will be measured for height and weight by the school nurse, although maybe I am dating myself, and each step of progress will be recorded on a chart. If they are not making progress a problem will be noted and a remedy suggested. If the remedy does not work a more serious problem will be noted and more action taken to correct it. Each step of the way there will be a checkup for progress made.

Christians need checkups as well. We need to evaluate if we are growing as we should. We need a guideline or checklist of proper and adequate development. If we didn't have these check lists for our children we wouldn't know if they were developing normally or not. If we don't have an appropriate set of goals for our Christian life we won't know if we are developing correctly or not either.

Peter told us to desire the pure milk of the word that we might grow thereby. Do we? How would we rate our Bible reading and study patterns for the past year? Better or worse than the year before? Are we becoming more Christ like? Another measure is related to the church. Christ loved the church and gave Himself for it. (Ephesians 5:25) What is our attitude toward the body of believers, the church? Is it secondary in our life? Do we love it like Christ did and set aside other things for it? Is this better or worse than our response to it a year ago? A third measure is how is our giving doing? If Christ loved the church and gave Himself for it, how is our giving to it? Do we trust Him more to take care of us than before and therefore entrust Him with more of our wealth? Is there growth there?

Could we expect our children to do well if they only attended school half the days it was in session? Can we expect to grow if we attend to the things of God only half the time? There are truly yardsticks by which we can measure our growth and development in our spiritual life. Paul admonishes the Corinthians to "examine yourselves as to whether you are in the faith. Test yourselves." (II Corinthians 13:5)

I look at Molly and am pleased at how far she has come since she became "my dog". My beloved bride sees the glass more like half empty. I'll accept half empty as a step in the right direction. When we got her there was a hole in the bottom of the glass. She is growing and developing. We will work on reaching her potential. Each of us in Christ must assume the same responsibility and grow up into Him, our living head.

CHAPTER TWELVE

"Beloved, let us love one another, for love is of God; and everyone
that loves is born of God and knows God."
I John 4:7

I know that Molly has some growth to do in certain areas. A well trained dog can understand and respond to more than three words. It can walk regularly on a loose leash and not just when it is in the mood to do so. Molly is a glass half full in some areas, but in one area she is a glass overflowing. It is one of those difficult to measure intangibles, but it is clearly seen. Molly is a lover.

A neighbor up the street has a very well behaved dog. They also have two signs on their yard. One is beware of dog. Their dog is big and has a deep voiced bark. I suppose one could be intimidated by it. The other sign is "Beware: Dog has licker license." When we walk by their house it just lays there or rolls over and looks at us. The dog next door to it and the one across the street are barking up a storm and attacking their fences, but not this one. Molly looks at him with a wistful look that seems to say, "Can I come in and play with you?" That dog is a lover and Molly knows it.

There are basic activities that can measure our growth in our spiritual life. We can evaluate by specific means whether we are spending time daily in God's Word. We can assess if our commitment to know and study it is growing or waning. We can measure if we are attending church and Sunday school faithfully. (That would be faithfully by a measure of regular consistency, not faithfully when it is convenient.) We can look into our bank records and see what place we esteem the work of Christ in our budget. These are tangible and measurable issues.

We cannot escape basics. Few children start in the fifth grade. When we get to the fifth grade we still use the basics we learned in the first grade. We don't discard them because we have moved on. We can't say, "Well, I attended church regularly for years, but I have moved beyond that now." We can't say, "Well, I read my Bible plenty in the past. I know it well enough." That is like saying that now that I know how to do long division I don't need to do two plus two anymore. Long division doesn't work without two plus two. We cannot discard the basic principles of Christian growth because we are not a new Christian anymore.

Growth in education is cumulative. It is the same in our Christian life. Peter says in II Peter 1:5-7, "But also for this reason, *giving all diligence*, **ADD** to your faith virtue, to virtue knowledge, to knowledge self-control, to self-control perseverance, to perseverance godliness, to godliness brotherly kindness, and to brotherly kindness love."

Two items at the start of that passage are critical. First is that we are to be diligent to do these things. To grow is to grip our life. Secondly is to ADD on one thing to another. Never does is suggest that one item is replaced by another or that we forget the basics.

The first list we used was elementary stuff. The Bible commands them and insists their constant necessity, but they are elementary. Church attendance, Bible reading and priority giving are not something we are to wait to learn later in our Christian life. They are the rudimentary issues. We can measure them and take stock of our spiritual health on a very basic level.

I have some pastor friends who preach on what they call the big five: church attendance, Bible reading, tithing, praying and witnessing. That is all they ever preach on. They tell me that when their people get the basics they will go on to another topic. Dearly beloved, it is important to get the basics, but the Scriptures tell us to build upon them - to build, add and grow. The basics are purely obedient faith, a faith that says, "We believe, therefore we do". Through the facility of these basics we are to learn, develop, mature, add and grow.

Peter lists seven things we are to add to our basic obedient faith: virtue, knowledge, self-control, perseverance, godliness, brotherly kindness and love. The last in this list of maturing Christian characteristics is love. This is an area in which Molly's cup is overflowing. She has a Master's Degree in Love.

Her love is first and foremost shown to her family. Since this is a parable and since her family is that new home into which she has been adopted, it is clear that her family to whom she demonstrates love is not her natural or birth family. She has this love attachment to her family of grace. For us, that would be the children of God, the body of Christ, the church of the redeemed, the family of God's grace.

Jesus, Peter, Paul, John and the author of Hebrews all stress the need for this special love relationship in the church family to be a dominant factor in open evidence in our life. Let us look briefly at the comments of each.

Jesus: "By this all men will know that you are my disciples if you have love for one another." John 13:35

Peter: "Since you have purified your souls in obeying the truth through the Spirit in sincere love of the brethren, love one another fervently with a pure heart." I Peter 1:22

Paul: "Be kindly affectionate to one another with brotherly love, in honor giving preference to one another." Romans 12:10

Hebrews: "Let brotherly love continue." Hebrews 13:1

John: "If someone says, 'I love God', and hates his brother, he is a liar; for he who does not love his brother whom he has seen, how can he love God whom he hasn't seen?" I John 4:20

It is an old and abused statement that charity begins at home. If we use charity in the King James sense of "faith, hope and charity and the greatest of these is charity", which today is translated love, then it is a true statement. Love does begin at home and there should be genuine love for our natural family. But there is also a new family and that love must also be genuine, evident and ever increasing.

Pastors hear a lot of things that would sadden the average heart. "I love this church; it's just the people that I can't stand." There is a statement that has often been repeated. It is tweaked in one way or another, but the meaning remains the same. "We don't sit on that side of the church . . . well, because . . ." and then a casual glance is offered in the direction of one or more people who do sit on that side of the church.

The pastor himself is often the focal point of this loveless conversation. Roast pastor has always been a common entrée at the Sunday dinner table of "good" Christians. It could be roast deacon, roast usher, roast Sunday school teacher or roast "lady with the big hat who sat in front of me". Early Christians were often accused of cannibalism because of the misperception of the lost community about the reality of the Lord's Table. While that error has been laid to rest, the reality of verbal cannibalism from a heart of impure love is all too truly common in our church communities.

In a very pointed comment Paul said, "Let love be without hypocrisy". (Rom. 12:9) The people that we "roast" are the people that we greeted, smiled at and, on communion Sunday, the one's with whom we shared the cup of the Lord. We broke bread, we sang *"We Are One in the Bond of Love"*, and then we roasted the person or the parson at our noon meal. Further, for the rest of the week we failed to join in any meaningful love relationship with anyone with whom we shared the fellowship of Word and prayer.

Do we have to wonder, seriously wonder, why the world

thinks the Christian message is a joke? Jesus said that all men would know we were his disciples by the love we openly showed to one another. We cannot show love if we don't get together. We can't show love if we don't get outside ourselves. We can't show love in our absence from one another from week to week, or in the case of many today whose attendance is so sporadic, from month to month.

John says, "My little children, let us not love in word or in tongue, but in deed and in truth." (I John 3:18) Our love life is lacking, seriously lacking. Our true commitment to the body of Christ is almost vaporous. The ecstasy and joy of seeing other believers, being with other believers and communing with other believers is a very rare commodity. Paul says to the Thessalonians, "For what is our hope, or joy, or crown of rejoicing? Is it not even you . . ." (I Thessalonians 2:19)

When I walk in the door there is someone waiting for me. She is wagging her tail and jumping up and down and chasing me all around the house. She is eager to see me even if I have just been gone five minutes. She is that way with every single member of my family and extended family. Some of them don't even like her, but she wants to sit next to them on the couch as much as those who love her in return. She roasts no one and loves everyone in the family. She is an example of Christian maturity that should challenge every believer. "Beloved, let us love one another."

CHAPTER THIRTEEN

"Beware of false prophets, who come to you in sheep's clothing, but
inwardly are ravenous wolves."
Matthew 7:15

Don't be fooled, Molly doesn't wag her tail for just anybody. She knows that she is a dog with responsibility. She has her "pack" to defend, her turf to keep safe and sometimes just a good hard bark to let out. She's a lover with an attitude.

That attitude would be caution. She is not an aggressive dog. Molly doesn't go looking for trouble. She is not mean. She is also not anyone's marshmallow. People with good common sense stop at the door when they meet her. She has given them every reason to do so by the time they have come up the steps. She wants to know who is coming and if it is OK to let them in. With the Master's permission she turns from caution to welcome.

God told the Israelites under both Moses and Joshua that they were to destroy all the people who dwelt within the land that God was giving them. One tribe in the land, the Gibeonites, knew that God meant business and that He would back Israel's army to achieve that end. They sent emissaries to the camp of the Israelites with a tricky plan. They took along worn out garments and moldy food. They told the Israelites that they had come from a far distant land and wanted to make peace. The Israelites agreed, but in chapter 9 verse 14 it states, "but they did not ask counsel of the Lord."

The Israelites were not cautious. They did not "beware". The result was that they ended up with pagan idolaters, the very people that God had already assigned to destruction, living right in the midst of their camp. This was the beginning of centuries of trouble marked by everything from compromise to full participation in the sins of the people surrounding them. Had they asked counsel of God it would have greatly brightened their future. They needed a watchdog at the door to sniff out the enemy and protect their land. They needed that dog to only allow in those OK'd by the Master.

What Molly does for my house and family, we need to be spiritually tuned to do in our Christian lives. Jesus warned of false prophets. Paul warned of false teachers and the "dogs" of the circumcision. Peter warned of the great satanic lion. John warned us to test the spirits. Moses warned of people who would rise up and teach Israel to walk in a way contrary to God. Jeremiah and Ezekiel warned against the false prophets who were preaching at the same time as they. It seems that we need a spiritual watchdog.

Our adversary has been described as "ravenous wolves in sheep's clothing" by Christ, "dogs" by Paul, a "roaring lion" by Peter, those who have "crept in unnoticed" by Jude and "an angel of light" by Paul. With so many warnings and so many descriptions of the enemy one would expect the church to be ever vigilant. Yet error runs rampant in the modern church from legalism to liberalism, from experientialism to humanism, from utter indifference to sin to nearly utter separation from worldly contact. The question must be posed, how did all this get in here? The answer, short and sweet, there has been no spiritual watchdog.

Jesus took three Disciples with him to a corner of the garden to pray on the night before His crucifixion. He told them to watch and pray. This is the same word used by Peter when he told the church to be vigilant against Satan. In this passage we find one key to a good spiritual watchdog – they are people of prayer. Jesus told those disciples that if they didn't pray they would fall prey to temptation and the flesh. I don't know what he told the three to pray, but we need to pray, "Lord, keep me alert to Satan's attacks." From the Lord's model prayer we pray, "Deliver us from evil (or the evil one)."

The three Disciples fell asleep and fled when the mob arrived. We fall asleep and are absent without leave when Satan walks in the door of the church with error in doctrine and practice.

The first answer of how all this error got into the church was that we didn't stay awake in prayer. Prayer may have been neglected or it may have become a ritual or a formal practice, but we weren't earnest in prayer to be kept from the evil one. Like the Israelites when confronted by the Gibeonites, we weren't really asking God's counsel.

Another way that error crept in was that we couldn't discern that it was error. In America today there is more access to tools of biblical research and study than at any time in history. Sadly there is also less use of these tools by the average Christian than at any time in history. A secular magazine once described modern American Christianity as being a lake a mile wide and an inch deep. We are a nation which professes great faith and is overwhelmingly ignorant of spiritual truth. We are a church that is ripe for error.

In Acts 17:11 Luke describes the people of Berea as "more fair minded than those in Thessalonica, in that they received the Word with all readiness and searched the Scriptures daily to find out whether these things were so." They didn't just hear the word, they checked it out. Day in and day out they were in their Bibles and could check out to see if they were hearing truth or error. The family altar, a once common institution in the Christian home, a time of united family Bible reading and prayer, is now a nearly extinct species of elementary Christian conduct.

When I was ten our church announced a special prize to the person who had most often read through their Bibles from Genesis to Revelation. On the night of the awarding of the prize (evening services now also being past tense in most congregations) there was a sizeable crowd. If you have read through your Bible at least once, please stand, the minister directed. No adult was left sitting. Even some teens were standing. Five times – remain standing, he said. The teens all sat but over ninety percent of the adults were still up. Ten times – remain standing, he said. It started to thin a little. Twenty times – remain standing, he said. Twenty percent of the people were still up. I was an awe struck little boy. The winner was 103 times. I knew that lady and I believed it without a doubt. Today it is estimated that only five percent of all Christians read their Bibles daily and that only a fraction of those have read it all.

The second watchdog is asleep and error is creeping in. My pastor friends who only emphasize the "big 5" would feel greatly justified in their choice of topic. We can't have virtue or knowledge or godliness without Bible reading and prayer.

Molly would be barking up a storm by now. If someone even walks on the sidewalk outside our fence after midnight she lets out a hew and cry. She listens, she smells and she reacts. It is hard to creep in unnoticed when there is a watchdog on duty.

There is a third reason, also part of the "big 5" that accounts for error. Paul tells the Ephesians that Christ gave the church pastors and teachers for "the equipping of the saints . . . for the edifying of the body . . . that we should no longer be children tossed to and fro and carried about with every wind of doctrine, by the trickery of men, in the cunning craftiness of deceitful plotting." (Ephesians 4:12-14) We are a church that has become exceedingly casual, almost indifferent, about regular church attendance. If the pastor is to protect the flock from error and they only hear three fourths or one half or one third of all the messages, how will they learn to discern truth from error? The author of Hebrews challenges us, "Not forsaking the assembling of ourselves together, as is the manner of some, but exhorting one another and so much more as you see the Day approaching." (Hebrews 10:25)

If we don't attend the preaching of the Word, study the Word and pray for guidance from the Word and protection from the evil one, then we will be like a blind and deaf dog that has a broken nose. We will eat any bit of poison fed to us by any hand. The wolf doesn't come as a wolf; it comes dressed in sheep's clothing. The good sheep dog, however, is alert and smells it out.

Molly, remember is maybe a border collie. She tends to the sheep and smells out the wolf. Or maybe she is the Karelian Bear dog. Then she is working with David as he protects the lambs of his flock from the lion and the bear. She is a working dog. Most of the time she seems to be working on a nap, but the second a strange noise occurs, or the second the gate opens or the second there is the tread of an unknown step on the back porch, she is totally alert.

The Israelites, when confronted by the Gibeonites, could not plead alertness. The Disciples, when Jesus came back to them and found them sleeping, could not plead alertness. The readers of Jude who had let ungodly men creep in unnoticed could not plead alertness. The church through the ages has not just seemed to be taking a nap; it has been asleep at the wheel. We have let in all manner of intruders that the Master would rather we had kept out. We need a lesson from Molly – guard the house and listen for the Master's OK before you let just anyone in.

CHAPTER FOURTEEN

"You are our epistle written in our hearts, known and read
by all men."
II Corinthians 3:2

When I was a child growing up in Sunday school and vacation Bible school, I had a favorite song. "Oh be careful little hands what you do, Oh be careful little hands what you do. For your Father up above is looking down in love, so be careful little hands what you do." It has rather gone out of vogue, but I still love to sing it. Be careful little hands, little feet, little eyes, little ears, and little tongue, yes, be careful. Someone is watching.

While the song expressly says that God is watching, someone else is watching. That would be the world around us. Paul expressed this to the Corinthians when he told them that they were an epistle or letter known and read by all men. Sometimes we think our pastor is watching or the church snoop is watching or the neighborhood snoop is watching, but in reality more people than that are watching. Molly has taught me that a lot of people are watching.

On a formerly taken evening route I would often stop and chat with a man who kept a beautiful yard. If he wasn't out in his yard I didn't stop at his door and look for him, but if he was then we chatted. It was never long or meaningful conversation, but it was a connection. A few blocks past his house, and the only way to get back to mine, was a particularly rough area where two big dogs routinely jumped over their four foot fence and came after me and Molly. After much swearing and threatening by their owners they usually ran off in another direction. I got tired of that routine and changed my route.

A few months later I thought I would try it again and see if those horrible dogs had been more properly restrained. As I got to the house where my chatting companion lived he said, "Where have you been? I haven't seen you for a long time?" I explained about the dogs up the street and he knew the house well. He expressed his sorrow about not seeing me, and Molly and I went on. The dogs were still not restrained and I haven't been back that way since.

A simple encounter with a man I didn't know had impacted his life. It may not have been an atomic impact, but he looked for me. A small chat, a spoken word, a routine passage by his house had not gone unnoticed. He knew when I would be by that spot each day. He had watched me. He was only one of many.

I was walking Molly one morning on our usual route when I met an elderly woman coming toward us. I greeted her and expected in return the half nod and smile received from most people, but she stopped. I stopped. "I see you go by my window every morning," she said. "I watch you and your beautiful dog go by every day." We chatted for a while and I went on my way.

While we walked the thought just kept running through my mind, "Every day she is watching me. That is both comforting and carries a great responsibility." I am comforted that in our neighborhood, as rough as it can be, that we are being watched over by seemingly anonymous observers. We are not alone out on the street. Now I will occasionally catch glimpses of this no longer anonymous watcher at the window of her apartment and wave to her in the mornings as we go by. She is a quiet "friend" in a potentially hostile world.

But that watching also comes with a responsibility. What is my conduct like every morning? When Molly has pushed me past the limits of my patience, how am I responding? "My Father up above is looking down in love" and so is the neighborhood. The neighborhood may not be nearly as loving as God in its observing, but they are still there, day by day, watching me go by.

One evening my beloved bride and I were walking Molly along the "new" evening route when a lady began chasing us down the street. In our neighborhood that may not always be a good thing. A teenage girl had been shot on that exact corner just a month before. In all honesty I didn't know that the lady was chasing us down the street. I am very hard of hearing and I didn't hear her yelling after us. The rush of traffic drowned out all other sounds for me.

Molly was pulling me on the right side and my beloved bride started pulling me on the left side. Which was the greater concern? Molly pulling to get at some garbage tossed by the side of the street or my beloved bride tugging on my arm, who needed me more? Seeing nothing remotely edible within the next three feet and wondering what had made my bride so upset, I asked her with utmost kindness, "What!?"

"There is a lady chasing us down the street and yelling at us," she replied. I turned around and sure enough, there was. A seemingly maniacal woman chasing after us from the front door of a bar seemed a bit disconcerting. We stopped, turned to face her and waited with smiling faces.

When she came up to us she burst out, "What kind of dog is that? She is beautiful!" To be honest I just looked at her dumbfounded. "You chased me screaming down the street just to ask what kind of dog I have?" was pounding in my head, but I wasn't going to say it. I am, after all, an epistle of the grace of God known and read by all men. I needed to say something more gracious.

"Thank you."

"I watch you go by every day and I admire your dog so much. She is such a well behaved dog." (At which point I thought she might have been roaring drunk – considering where she had just come from and all.) "I wish my dog would behave like that." By this time she was right in front of me and she didn't smell of alcohol at all. She must have had a very bad dog.

As we visited she shared a number of things she had noticed about Molly during all those evenings that we had walked by. She had noticed the short leash we now use that helps her walk more obediently. She had noticed that the leash was often slack. She had noticed certain features about Molly. She had been watching, quite obviously, for some time. It turned out that she lived in the apartment above the bar. We assured her that her dog would grow up and become better behaved if she just kept up the things she was doing to train it. Then off we went.

We hadn't walked more than a hundred feet down the street when a car honked at us and the passenger called out the window, "That's a beautiful dog you have there."

We are being watched. Whether it is a passing moment like the car driving by or it is the ongoing observation of people on their porches or from their apartment windows, we are being watched. We are being watched by people we don't know and by people we do. We are being watched from the most unlikely places – an apartment over a bar. Our lives are being scrutinized by the world.

People first notice us for a variety of reasons. We cannot even guess at what all of them might be. It will be a reason that is personal to them individually. To someone who loves children, they might notice us because of our children. To someone who loves dogs they might notice us because of our dog. To someone who is lonely they might notice us because we offered a simple smile and hello.

They notice us and then they watch us. Finally they read us. It may be a short story of a few moments or a novel of long observation. What do they read in us? They might see that while the man of sin inside of me is saying, "Just throttle this dog", the man of grace isn't doing so. They don't hear the voice in my head just the grace of Christ in my response.

What they need to see in us is the grace of God. They don't need to see another drunk reeling down the street swearing at his children and his dog. There is enough abuse of anything and anyone to numb us all. What they need to see is something different. Why? Because, just maybe, someday they will see that we are a Christian. They may ask, "Why are you this way?"

Maybe it is the neighbor three doors down who sees you pull out of your driveway each Sunday morning and they can say, "Oh, that is why they act that way." Let us not let them say, "Oh my! And they act THAT WAY!!" We don't know how much is observed or what all the conclusions will be. We just need to always remember that we are being observed. What conclusions about Christ do we want people to draw from the observations they make. Let us make our "books" good clean reading for the world around us and then the Father up above who is looking down in love will always be pleased with us.

CHAPTER FIFTEEN

"He who did not spare His Own Son, but delivered Him up for us all, how shall He not with Him also freely give us all things?"
Romans 8:32

I have pastored churches for a long time. During those many years I have met a lot of people with a lot of strange and sad doctrines. One of the saddest is the idea that once God has taken care of our salvation, we are pretty much on our own. No one really articulates it that way, but after talking around the issue and through the issue and about the issue, that is the general conclusion. It was mighty nice of God to save them, but since He is a busy Guy He can't really be bothered by all the things of our life. He has given us the most important thing; we really don't need to ask Him or expect from Him anything else.

I just didn't love my dog when I rescued her from imminent death, I love her now. Actually, not being God, I didn't really love her when I rescued her, I just did it. God, on the other hand, loved us before He saved us. He loved us from the foundation of the world. That was when Christ was crucified in the eternal purpose of God. The event happened in history. The plan and purpose of that event was set before God placed man on this earth. God was determined to show His eternal grace by loving us when He knew we would be sinners and while we were sinners. So, God's love predates our rescue in time to the eternal plan of the triune God for our salvation in pre-history. He truly loved us when He rescued us from certain death and judgment, and He loves us now.

What does that mean for our life? Let us think of our own children. They are easier to use as an illustration than Molly. We wanted children so we took the necessary action to have children. We loved them in planning for them. We loved them in the conception of them. We loved them in the incubation of them. We loved them at birth. We love them as they grow up. We love them as they mess up our house. We love them as they run amok and often break our hearts. We loved them before they were and we love them after they come to us.

My love for Molly didn't come until later. That doesn't, however, diminish how much I care for my dog. Since I care for my dog, and since we care for our children, our love for them does not stop at the point of birth. Neither does God's love for us, His care for us and His intimate interest in us wane with time. If He was so concerned for me that He would have His Son die for me when I wasn't His child, how much more concerned for me is He now that I am His child? The latter love is no less than the saving love.

When Molly came to us she did so with a beat up old collar and leash. I got her a nice bright new pink collar and leash which she proceeded to eat up. I got her another one. I got her a nice pretty pink bandana to tie around her neck. She hates it, of course, and we only use it for dress up occasions like going to the nursing home. She didn't just come to my house and become my dog; she came to my house, became my dog and got the nice things that I wanted to give her.

Ditto for God. We come to God at His invitation and He lavishes on us the riches of Christ Jesus with whom we are joint heirs. Let us consider briefly some of the many things that He gives to us.

He exchanged our ragged and filthy robes of sin for the

blood washed robes of righteousness in Jesus Christ. Isaiah tells us that "all our righteousnesses are like filthy rags" (Isaiah 64:6). Paul says that "He made Him who knew no sin to be sin for us, that we might become the righteousness of God in Him." (II Corinthians 5:21) We don't belong in filthy rags of sin; we are children of the God of the universe. He gave us Christ's robe of righteousness and He wants us to wear it, just like I want Molly to wear her pretty pink collar and go about on her pretty pink lead.

He gives us the promise of answered prayer. Jesus said, "For everyone who asks receives, and he who seeks finds, and to him who knocks it shall be opened." (Matthew 7:8) If Molly wants to play tug-of-war I don't say, "Listen, Dog, I gave you a nice warm house, now leave me alone." If she brings me the tug-of-war rope we will play. Of course, there are exceptions. I won't play tug-of-war on Sunday mornings when I am dressed for church. God won't play Santa Claus and give us whatever we ask for. The passage about asking and receiving is about needs, not wants and about the right responsibilities of the Father and not about the greed of the child.

In Ephesians 1:17 Paul prays that God will give the believers wisdom and knowledge and in verse 18 he adds a prayer for understanding of God. Why do we need this? Simply because our ways are not His ways (Isaiah 55:8) If we go on through our lives using just our own wisdom we will get no further along the right path than we did before we repented of that failure and came to Him. To gain that knowledge and understanding and wisdom Paul repeatedly emphasizes that we need to be in the Word of God and to have our minds renewed. Without that renewal we will continue to be conformed to this world. Paul makes it plain "be not conformed to this world, but be transformed by the renewing of your mind, that you may prove what is that good and acceptable and perfect will of God." (Romans 12:2) As we did not get salvation until we believed, so we don't just get wisdom without pursuing it God's way.

What else did He give us? Paul goes on in Ephesians 1 and prays that we will grasp the hope of His calling. Men offer hope and they never deliver. God offers hope and He never fails. The hope of our calling is so broad that it encompasses our whole position as children of God, children of His care now, His presence now and a home with Him forever. This hope is driven by faith in God and when we accept the reality of the things that we cannot see we will live the victorious Christian life that is portrayed in Hebrews 11. All the heroes of the faith had faith driven hope that made them live lives that we should all aspire to have.

Paul adds in his prayer in Ephesians 1:19 that we should grasp the exceeding greatness of His power toward us. A tornado touched down about twenty miles northwest of us and continued on the ground going northwest for over twenty more miles. A number of people were killed. One town was devastated and three other communities and their rural environs greatly damaged. Debris from that tornado ended up landing in yards and fields over a hundred miles away. That was power displayed in a negative way.

God's power toward us is unfathomably more powerful than that tornado, but it should be displayed in positive ways. As the power of earth took lives, the power of God in us should make people come alive. As the power of earth brought devastation the power of God in us should bring edification of the saints and comfort to the world. As the power of this world was felt at great distance, the power of God in changing our lives should be noted near and far. Paul wrote to the Thessalonians and said, "For from you the Word of the Lord has sounded forth, not only in Macedonia and Achaia, but also in every place. Your faith toward God has gone out, so that we do not need to say anything. For they themselves declare concerning us what manner of entry we had to you, and how you turned to God from idols to serve the living and true God." (I Thessalonians 1:8-9) The power of God that changed them changed everything around them. That is the power of God to us in Jesus Christ.

On top of all these things, and these are barely touching the many things that He keeps on giving us daily, He has given us the assurance of His ongoing care and presence. In Romans 8 where Paul has stated that He will freely give us all things, he goes on to state the obvious. "Who shall separate us from the love of Christ?" (8:35) He adds this profound promise, "For I am persuaded that neither death nor life, nor angels nor principalities *(including Satan)* nor powers, nor things present nor things to come, nor height nor depth, nor any created thing *(we are created things so that includes us)* shall be able to separate us from the love of God which is in Christ Jesus our Lord." (8:38-39)

On our short list God has given us robes of righteousness, answered prayer, access to wisdom, knowledge and understanding, true hope, power to change ourselves and our environment for Him and the certain assurance of His never failing love for us. This is just the short list. The complete list of all that He has given us, what He is and wants to give us and what He will give us in the future are found on almost each page from Genesis to Revelation.

This rather makes the pink collar, leash and bandana I gave to Molly pale by comparison, doesn't it? And yet, I am not God. I give Molly things and take care of her and see that she is healthy and fed because she is my dog. My care for her did not stop when I adopted her. It just began. God's care for us is like that. He gave Jesus for our salvation and keeps giving us things in Jesus every day. He is the wonderful God!

CHAPTER SIXTEEN

"And also let grain from the bundles fall purposely for her; leave it
that she may glean, and do not rebuke her."
Ruth 2:16

This is one of my absolute favorite passages of Scripture. Read it twice; then read it twice more again. Meditate on it. Read it. Weep. At this point in reading through the book of Ruth I always begin to cry. It doesn't matter that I have read the text fifty or more times and know what is going to happen next. Read it. Meditate on it. Weep.

This is Jesus (Boaz) speaking to his loyal servants to leave ON PURPOSE grain to fall from their bag that the unclean outsider (Ruth) who is condemned by heritage may have enough to eat and thrive. There will not only be enough for her but for her family as well. God's provision is ON PURPOSE! God's provision is by handfuls on purpose. It isn't meager or a tad. It isn't skimpy or insufficient to do more than barely survive. It is handfuls ON PURPOSE.

Yes, this relates to Molly. Because this is one of my favorite passages of Scripture I think of it in many situations. Molly often inspires the recollection of this passage. She is the condemned outsider. I am the lord, her savior. Please notice the lower case "l" and "s".

How does this play out? We are sitting at the table and Molly saunters into the kitchen. She looks at me with her big brown eyes and sighs. Yes, she actually sighs. Then she comes to me and lays her head on my thigh and rolls her eyes up at me. There are many in my family who say, "Tell the beggar to go away." They are probably right in a sense of pure etiquette. She does, after all, smell like a dog even when she is freshly bathed. Also, no one wants her to wander from my place at the table to theirs. No one except the grandchildren, that is. They love feeding Molly at the table. That is one more small reason their parents often object, I suppose. However, I digress. She is looking at me with a clear sense of anticipation. In Christian circles we call that prayer. I am her lord and master. She is beseeching me for a special boon, an ort, a simple scrap of the end of a dinner roll. What would Jesus do?

I love my dog. I feel a great sense of responsibility for my dog. I feed her well. I provide her with fresh water when her bowl is only half empty. She is not starving or dying of thirst. She is not pleading for daily bread. She is pleading for something special. I give her that end of the dinner roll. She wags her tail. She goes to the grandchildren for a bigger bite. She is a dog.

That's what Ruth was, a dog. She was of a nation that God had specifically put on the "out" list from the blessings of the children of Israel. I am sure that being good sons of Israel Boaz's workers thought of her as a dog and thought of Boaz as touched by too much sun when he said, "Let grain from the bundles fall purposely for her." Not only that but he had fed her at *their* table. Not only that, but she had been told that she could drink from *their* water pitcher. She, a dog of Moab!

What did Boaz do? It was in his power to treat her like a dog or to be gracious to her. He could have left her the tiniest scraps that his workers missed in the fields. He could have excluded her from the table where they ate and from the water that they drank. He could have done so, but he didn't. He commanded his servants to take heads of grain and drop them purposely in her path. He commanded them to move down the table a little to let her have a place to sit. He commanded them to draw enough water for her to drink as well. He did not turn her away!

Jesus confronted a similar situation when He was in the region of Sidon in Matthew chapter 15. A Canaanite woman came up to Him and His Disciples and asked for a miracle. He at first denied her request. That met with the Disciples expectations. She was a Canaanite, a dog. Jesus even calls her a dog. Check out verse 26 of chapter 15, "It is not good to take the children's bread and throw it to the little dogs." Technically she should be dead. God had commanded the children of Israel to destroy all the Canaanites. They didn't. So now Jesus is confronted by an unclean woman, a woman who is condemned by birth and who wants a miracle.

She got it. She recognized her true status. She was a dog. She was unworthy. But she knew and believed that Christ, the Son of God, Jesus the Man in front of her, was able to meet her request and was gracious. She said to Him, "Yes, Lord, yet even the little dogs eat the crumbs which fall from their master's table." She calls Him Lord and Master and Jesus responds by saying, "Woman, great is your faith" and giving her the miracle. She did not go away empty handed. She got plenty from the Lord for herself and for her family.

When we recognize the true nature of our own unworthiness, when we recognize the actual depravity of our sin condition, when we do this and come to Jesus and say, "Yes, Lord, I am unworthy, but Your blood was shed for sinners", then we can be assured that He will not turn us away. He will not give us just the ort for the moment. He will give us the bread that feeds to eternity and the living water of life that will constantly refresh our soul. And then, as we walk along the way He will give us handfuls on purpose to bless our soul and our life. God is a great dog owner and I am very glad that I am His dog.

So I try to be a great dog owner. The result: Molly is a bit pampered perhaps. Maybe she is spoiled. Some people tell me so. I don't believe a word of it. She is my dog and I give her good things. Would Christ do less for us? I meet her needs sufficiently and beyond. I can look myself honestly in the mirror and state that I have not reduced my giving to mission work or other Christian ministry since getting Molly. In fact, I have increased it. She is not detracting me from the work of God either directly or vicariously. I simply am trying to be a great dog owner.

Molly's tidbits at the table are only a part of her balanced diet. She really likes the end of mealtime. As I give her scraps from the meal I still think of the handfuls on purpose of Christ. As I watch her wag her tail and jump around in anticipation of something as simple as a leftover broccoli crown or a few green beans I am reminded of the great graciousness of God to me. (Just a note here, the only things that Molly doesn't like is lettuce and grapes.)

Molly's regular food is another challenge. When I go to the store and walk through the dog food aisle I am confronted by many choices. There are fifty pound bags of store brands for a dollar or two less than forty pound bags of food recommended by our vet. Again I think of handfuls on purpose. I think of the promise of Romans 8 where God will withhold no good thing from us since He has already not withheld Christ from us. It is a simple everyday situation where I am confronted by the truth of God's Word to me as His child. Having Molly has confronted me with ideas and challenges that I never considered until God put them in perspective to me through the parables He taught me on our walks.

I can never do for Molly what God can do for me. His resources are unlimited and His knowledge is complete. If it is harmful to me He doesn't hand it out with handfuls on purpose. He knows better. I am guided by human reasoning of divine principles. He is simply the Divine. He can make no mistakes. I can and do make lots of them. God is in the right in all things while I still see through a glass darkly. No, God is a far better owner than I will ever be.

It is God's handfuls on purpose that I try to grasp. How does this all work? How can and should it play out in my life? There were many gleaners in the fields of ancient Israel. It was God's law that they should be allowed to glean. It was beyond the letter of God's law that Boaz undertook the care of Ruth. Boaz's provision for Ruth went beyond his provision for other gleaners. There was not a general equality to all while there was always obedience to the nature and purpose of the law of gleaning for all. For Ruth there were handfuls on purpose.

Ruth had a known faith. She had abandoned her own false gods to follow Naomi and her God. Ruth had a known need. She and Naomi had no visible means of support beyond Ruth's meager gleanings. Ruth had a character of obedience. She was obedient to Naomi and to the law of gleaning. A young woman could have sought her opportunities in other ways, a fact that Boaz acknowledged to her. Was this behind the response of Boaz to Ruth?

If our love is to begin in the household of the faith, are these a basis to follow in giving our own handfuls on purpose? Handfuls on purpose are the act of the love of God being poured out. Let us consider what that means to us and consider what that could mean through us as well. More than Molly is waiting at the table of life.

CHAPTER SEVENTEEN

"Wherefore, lift up the hands which hang down,
and the feeble knees."
Hebrews 12:12

I am from the Midwest. I don't really mind a good hard winter. If it is 35 degrees below zero then it is minus 35, so be it. If I have to walk Molly when it is minus 35 then she gets walked. Just bundle up is the rule. But what if it is in the middle of nice snowy winter and then all of a sudden it is 40 degrees above zero? That I don't like. Suddenly the streets are full of slush and sidewalks are ponds between two banked sides of snow. What to wear on my feet is the major problem.

I have special footwear for walking Molly. For snow there are the springs that clip on the bottom of the shoe. For ice there are the spikes that clip on to the bottom of the shoe. Both of these fit on my insulated hiking boots. But what to wear when it is just slush? Neither the springs nor the spikes really work well. I also don't like wearing my insulated hiking boots even though they are waterproof. I hate walking through inches deep puddles in them. So, I have a pair of Duck Boots. (I have no idea why they are called "duck boots", but they are.)

The problem with duck boots is that they are larger than my regular hiking boots. Neither the springs nor spikes fit on them.

The second problem with duck boots is that they have no, I mean absolutely no traction. They are simply a formed rubber boot which is nicely insulted for outdoor wear where no traction is needed. On really slushy days I get out my duck boots. That is fine – unless . . . unless you need traction.

It was just such a nasty over warm day in a very snowy cold winter when I had to wear my duck boots to take Molly for her walk. The snow was nearly a foot deep on each side of the sidewalks being banked up there by multiple shovelings over the past month. Between these snow banks lay vast puddles of water that might extend down the sidewalk for 15 to 30 feet or more. Molly didn't care. I had my duck boots on and was ready to face it as it came. Unfortunately, it came in a most unplanned way.

Four blocks from our house we encountered just such a puddle. We had passed many already and this was "no big deal". Well, it was. At one point in the bottom of this little mini-lake was a sheet of frozen ice. I was in duck boots with no traction. The water was deep and the sheet of ice invisible. Before I even knew what was happening I had slipped. It wasn't a little slip. My feet went head high and my head went feet high, right onto the cement sidewalk. No, the inch of water provided no padding whatsoever.

Yes, I was knocked out, at least momentarily. I must have bounced because I ended up face down in the snow bank beside the sidewalk with my lower body prone in the mini-lake of ice water. My glasses were thrown off, my head ached in the back and had a cut in the front (still unexplained) and I simply couldn't move. And then I thought of Molly – did she run off? No, she didn't.

She was right there putting her face in mine urging me to sit up. A passing motorist had stopped in the street and was calling out to me, "Sir, are you OK, sir?" All my brain could think was, "Do I look OK?" She kept calling out the same thing until she kindly got out of her car and came over to help me. I thought a new thought, "Oh, no! Molly is going to attack her." Molly can be like that to strangers on the street. But Molly didn't. Molly sat down in the snow and watched this lady help me. She never growled or bared her teeth. She even seemed to help the lady pick me up and get me on my feet and over to a front stoop of a house to sit down again.

I was impressed. I have seen her lose her cool toward strangers that have approached me on the street before. She especially, for a completely unknown reason, can't seem to stand people on cell phones. This lady was calling 9-1-1 on her cell phone. Molly was completely unperturbed. She was at my knees with her paw in my lap and her nose in my face. When the ambulance arrived she even let the EMT approach me. He was in uniform and dogs are not always all that crazy about people in uniform. She sat and watched me and let him alone. She hopped in the ambulance with me and continued to let the EMT minister to me without any response from her. What a dog!

While I was groggy about many things I was actually noticing all this at the time. It made quite an impression on me. How much like Molly we all need to be. Amazingly, that was my thought at the time. Pastors must be wired like that or something. A good biblical illustration is always nice. Perhaps we should all be looking at life like that, but I can assure you that pastors are doing it even in the most bizarre circumstances.

How many people fall daily? I don't mean on the icy sidewalk. Our daughter-in-law is a doctor. She said the emergency room was very busy for those two days of melting temperatures. There are lots of falls on the ice in the winter. What I mean, is how many people fall, figuratively, every day? The answer would be far more than there are on the ice.

How many people then are like the lady who stopped and called out to me and then came and rescued me? How many are like Molly who stand by their friends and nudge them back onto their feet? How many stand by encouragingly while their friend recovers from their fall? How many lift up the hands which hang down and the feeble knees?

A common criticism of Christians is that people in churches seem more ready to judge us for the stupidity of falling down than are willing to help us get back up. Indeed on the Sunday after this incident several people were more critical of my being ill prepared to be on the ice than they were concerned about the injuries that I had received. Lack of Christian concern goes beyond just the allegorical applications.

Why are we like this? Why do people leave church after church with the same complaint? What is wrong with the modern Christian psyche that impels us to destroy our relationships instead of build them? I am not sure that there is an easy answer to the question, but there is an easy answer to the problem. Stop it!!!

There really is no simpler answer. When our children start to "act up" we say, "Stop it." When they don't, we amplify our voice and say, "Stop it now!!" We are good at telling people to "stop it" and we need to stop and listen to our own voices. Stop killing the wounded. A friend of mine is a Marine. He loves the corps' philosophy of never leaving a comrade behind. No wounded Marine needs to fear being abandoned by his squad. They hang in there together. They went in together and they will come out together. When we think of doing anything else we need to hear our parents' voices, our voices as parents, "Stop It NOW!!!"

God reminds us over and over and over again in His Word that we are all part of one another. The church though seemingly many is really just one. We are all parts of the body of Christ which is one body. If my toe hurts I don't take a hammer and hit it to make it hurt less. It is part of my body. If I hit it with a hammer I know that it will hurt more than it already does and that I too will hurt more than I already do. That is what it is like to part of the same body.

But we ignore this truth every day to the hurt of the body of

Christ as a whole and to the hurt of individual parts that are most hurting. I fell and ended up with a badly sprained wrist and a nasty concussion along with other bruises and cuts. I hurt. I hurt a lot. Molly stood beside me. Molly nudged me to get up. Molly was patient with those who came to my aid. She didn't bark or growl or try to intimidate them. She was quietly by my side the whole time. Molly displayed more Christ-likeness than many people in many churches every day. She openly showed that she was the adopted and loved member of the family.

We must begin the process of helping others with the simple realization that God has first helped us. When we could not save ourselves, He did it for us. He adopted us and made us part of His family. He embraced us when we were most unembraceable. And then He keeps us. He is not always busy amputating parts of His body because of some problem or other. He is busy trying to heal His body, tending and caring for it with all the compassion of the cross. He sends us to be like Him. He sends us to minister to those in need, not just the lost outside the church, but to the fellow members of Christ's body who are hurting.

He wants us to nudge our Christian brothers who have fallen to get back up in a standing position. He wants us to prod them back to walking. If we ignore everyone that falls we will soon discover that we are walking alone and that there is no one to assist us when we fall ourselves. Get your nose in their face, kindly and lovingly with all the compassion of Christ and lift up the fallen hands and week knees. Lick the wounds of your fellow member of Christ. Remember that even a dog has sense enough to do that and then live out your love for Christ in real ways to the really hurting.

CHAPTER EIGHTEEN

"And Aaron and Hur supported his hands, one on one side, and the other on the other side; and his hands were steady until the going down of the sun."
Exodus 17:12

I once had a job on the eighth floor of an office building. At the start of the work day I rode the elevator to that floor and began working. At my first break I walked down the 8 flights of stairs, walked over to the river front walkway and walked along the river front to circle back to the office building and walked back up the eight flights of stairs, got a drink and went back to work. During my lunch break and afternoon break I repeated the cycle. At day's end I walked down the stairs and walked the one mile across town to my house. I did this whether the weather was 80 degrees outside or 10 degrees. I hate to sit and I love to walk.

Vacation plans mean different things to different people, and I admit that I am a different people. When we make plans for vacation I search out new areas to go hiking. I have learned that if I take just one day from this pursuit to loll around a few small town specialty interest stores while my beloved bride window shops, then she is cool with the rest of the vacation being on the move through forests, fields, deserts or whatever might be the venue for that year's hiking vacation. (Isn't my bride just the finest woman any man ever had the opportunity to marry?)

But hiking isn't just for vacations. Any day that I can grab off is a good occasion to put on the hiking shoes. Our city has developed one of the best hiking trail systems around. It is over 50 miles long and extends in every direction and utilizes rivers, forests and open prairies as the primary backdrop for the trails. Our county parks system is also expanding its hiking trail opportunities. These extend into trails from other counties and give a good trail of over 50 miles in one direction through the fabulous Iowa countryside.

But, it's not just me that likes to walk. Molly loves going along on these excursions when we let her. We take along an extra bottle of water and a water dish and she is set to go. She is a good companion and she even proves her worth some days.

We were at a park with a very steep hill. I especially like the parks with steep hills. My beloved bride, as usual, was asking me to hold Molly's leash. Molly is an eager dog and my already long arms have grown longer since getting her. She pulls. No, she PULLS. Nothing has deterred her. We have tried multiple techniques and gizmos and nothing slows her down. She is a goer.

So, we have this steep hill and Molly and I and by bride are walking up it. Gradually I notice that it is just Molly and me walking up it. I turned around and my beloved was nearly 100 yards in the rear. We stopped and waited for her to catch up and began our ascent again. Soon she was far behind. I was baffled. My bride is a fairly decent walker though not a particularly good climber. But certainly, she wasn't that bad of a climber to fall so far behind so quickly. After a brief discussion of the matter I gave her Molly's leash and soon I found myself way behind on the trail. I had to jog up the trail to remain even close. Molly was doing all the work. We were along for the ride. Joint effort bore great success while working alone brought tiredness and an ever greater lagging behind.

The church of Jesus Christ is like that. As a pastor I am often asked why church A seems to be doing a more successful job than church B. If church B would just adopt that other church's music program, kids program, Sunday school curriculum, or whatever, would they then enjoy the same success? Every "build a church" system that is out there for the purchasing promises those results. I hate to tarnish anyone's system or seriously hurt anyone's sales, but there is really a completely different factor at work. It is not a system; it is simple obedience to biblical truth already given.

Successful churches have learned, or simply practice by chance, the greatest dynamic for success that will ever work in any church. They walk up the hill in tandem. They work together. Each one contributes his or her best to the operation. No one sits on the sidelines. The New Testament is replete with illustrations of this concept. We are one body with many parts. Try walking up the hill without any legs. It is a tougher go than using the legs. Try singing a song without any tongue. It is easier to sing with a tongue.

Try building a church by paying the pastor's salary and leaving the work to him. Soon he is tired and the church board is wondering if they made such a great choice in his selection. Other churches in the area seem to be outstripping them in "success". Result; send him to another convention to learn better and more successful techniques. Or maybe the church can call in a consultant with a "build your church" system and spend upwards of $1000 to try something new with the same pastor still taking point on all the activities.

We have bought into a world system that says "hire it done". God's system is simple and simply says, "Do it". Home Depot, Lowes, Menards are all successful at promoting do it yourself projects. Take the bull by the horns and remodel your own house. Do your own painting and do your own papering and do your own window installations and do, do, do, do it yourself. Still in our churches we expect someone else to do the doing for us. We expect to hire it done and forget about it until next week. We need to rethink our process, not our program.

Going up the hill with Molly was a joint venture. She did provide most of the legwork; that is true. But, I had the hand on the leash. Without my hand on the leash we would have had a lost dog and still had to struggle on our own up the steep hill. By passing Molly back and forth between us we were each able to catch our breath and keep up and get to the top. Shared work, shared responsibility and then shared success was the result.

This principle is as old as Moses. Moses and the children of Israel were in a real scrape. They were being attacked by some of the fiercest desert warriors around. Here is a band of former slaves now confronting a major enemy. Moses, Aaron and Hur go up on a hilltop to watch the battle progress. Moses raises his hands in a prayer to God and the Israelites prevail in battle. Moses' hands got tired and he lowered them and the Amalekites prevailed.

Up his hands went. Victory. Down his hands went. Defeat. It was a yo-yo of frustration. Then Aaron and Hur got smart. They put a stone seat under Moses and set him down. Then one of them took the right hand of Moses and the other took the left hand of Moses and they stood there the rest of the day holding up his hands. Victory was secured. They worked together. They didn't carp at Moses to hold his own hands up. They didn't run down to the congregation and say, "Moses can't keep his hands up and we are going to lose." They didn't say, "Let's get someone else up here who is stronger and can hold their hands up longer." No, they simply held his hands up. They worked together to solve the problem. Each part of the body did its part.

So what is it about church A that makes it more successful than church B? Well there could really be many things. They could be clearly tangible things or intangible things. But the first thing that needs to be asked and honestly answered is, are the people in church A working together better than the people in church B? Does church A have a "get it done" philosophy and church B a "hire it done" philosophy? Does church A try cooperation in labor and church B try gimmicks of labor? Are the board members of church A contributing work to the church and the board of church B contributing suggestions for work to be done at the church?

This needs to be an honest conversation in many churches. People need to be willing to examine what they are actually doing and how they are actually participating. It can be a painful exercise for some to discover that their greatest contributions have been their voices and not their efforts. Plans of inclusion must be formulated so that everyone can contribute to the whole more effectively. Responsibilities must be shared and not ignored by the designer of the responsibility only to be thrust upon the pastor in order to make sure things do get done. Tiredness and lagging behind will always result.

After our conversation on the side of that steep hill, it was discovered that the work was not being equally shared. She didn't want to hold the dog, but she didn't want to fall behind. To keep up my bride had to share in the leash of the dog. As we continued up the slope the leash became more and more a shared responsibility. Even Molly enjoyed the brief moments of rest as we changed her leash from hand to hand. In no time at all we were at the top, and we were there together. And who should lead us into this great discovery? A dog! God certainly couldn't make it any simpler than that.

CHAPTER NINETEEN

"That He might sanctify and cleanse it with the washing of water by the word."
Ephesians 5:26

Perhaps I have mentioned one or two times in this book that I love my dog. Actually there is a picture on my computer desk of Molly in a small frame. On the frame it says, "I love my dog." In case I am ever inclined to forget that I love my dog, there is a constant reminder for me that I do indeed love her. There she stands in the picture with her tail all nicely curled up over her back. She is staring straight at me. Her white bibbed front is freshly clean along with her nice white paws. Her stance is clearly anticipating me coming to do something with her – whether to play or walk or pet; she is ready.

Ephesians 5:25 says, "Christ loved the church and gave Himself for her." Verse 26 adds that He would clean her and then verse 27 adds, "That He might present it to Himself a glorious church, not having spot or wrinkle, or any such thing; but that it should be holy and without blemish." Molly is our parable, our visible lesson of what it means to be a Christian. Christ loves. Christ cleans us. Christ will present us to Himself clean and pure and ready as His bride. Christ loves, cleans, cares, tends, and is actively engaged with us as a groom with His bride or a master with a loved dog.

The picture that Paul paints of how we will be presented to Christ is far different from the one we see of ourselves honestly every day. Am I clean, holy, without blemish? Well, yes and no. That is the glory of being His and the problem of being human. In my picture of Molly she is always clean. I cannot add dirt to the picture. In my presence on my desk, she is always clean and ready for me. In earthly reality she is not always so. How can there be two realities that are both true?

Reality one is my presence and my throne. This is my computer chair. This is my computer desk. This is my work station. She is in front of me in this place. She is perfectly clean and ready and eager to do something with me. A good picture can capture the ideal. With computer enhancements people are always making themselves into something that they are not really. Pictures are altered to present the best possible image of what we want to be. But those pictures are not real. This one of Molly is. I had taken the time to prep her for this picture. There is no enhancement that was not made by effort of the master. It is not a disguise of herself that she sought. It is the perfect her – brushed, combed, sleek and clean – that I sought and labored to achieve.

Christ labored for us. He came into this world from His perfect heavenly home. He was born in a stable. He lived his childhood and early adulthood in obscurity until he was 30 years of age. Then, after such a protracted humiliation of the true King of kings, he began to labor publicly for us. The Gospel of Mark pictures the rushing servant busy about His Father's business of caring for the sheep of His fold.

There He is healing someone in one place then rushing to heal someone else in another. On the way He is teaching those around Him. He is feeding the multitudes while healing not just one but the multitudes. Then He is off to another place to do the same and the same again and again. He is so tired that He can fall asleep in a boat in the middle of a horrible storm and not be awakened but by the exertions of His friends to awaken Him. Along the path of His great charity and love He is scorned by the scornful and mocked by the ignorant. Still undaunted He works and labors on. He tells those around Him that He and they must labor while there is day to labor in. He tells them that there is a need for more laborers. Labor, labor and more labor fill His days and sleepless hours of laboring in prayer fill His nights.

But that is not the extent of His labor. He came unto His own and they rejected Him and despised Him. Ultimately they crucified Him and He entered His greatest labor. He died for the sins of the world. He died that His blood could make us clean. He died, the innocent for the guilty, so that His cleanness could replace our defilement and we could have new clean robes of righteousness to replace our dirty rags of sin. He labored up until He said to the Father, "It is finished" and then He died. He had finished all the labor that the Father had given Him to do for us.

But then He labored still. He descended to the dead and proclaimed that victory had been won for all who had died waiting for Him. Then He rose victoriously having done the great labor of defeating death and Satan's most fearsome hold on mankind.

Still His labor is not done. Though He sits on the Father's right hand, He labors still. He intercedes for us. He prays for us. He pleads His blood before the Father for us and keeps us pure in the Father's presence with the perfection of His own sacrifice for sin once for all made on the cross of Calvary. Christ is not idly twiddling His thumbs in heaven. No, He labors still on our behalf as He labored on our behalf when He was here among us. He labors to prepare a place for us and then will come and take us from all our labor to be with Him forever.

All that labor was done to make us clean and acceptable before the Father. The picture we have in heaven before the Father's throne is one of perfection and beauty. It is not falsely enhanced. It was taken with great care after great labor was put into the subject of the picture – us – to make us fit to have that picture taken. It is Molly looking at me all clean and brushed and eager. It is the product of much hard work on behalf of one who could not do the work herself. I washed her and it was a lot of work!

Molly is not naturally a clean dog. She is a dog. Left to herself she would be quite content to be a dirty dog. She gladly rolls in the dirt and the grass. She walks through mud puddles without the least care. And the things that she eats, well, she thinks that the dirtier a thing is the better it must be for her. She is a dirty dog. She is a dog.

We are people. How does God see us outside of Jesus Christ? Not at our best, and that is a fact. God tells Isaiah, "But we are all as an unclean thing, and all our righteousnesses are as filthy rags; and we all do fade as a leaf, and our iniquities, like the wind, have taken us away." What a picture. We are filthy rags at our very best moments. Just when we think that we are so great and God should be glad to have made such a fine specimen of humanity as us, well, He sees it differently.

Our most righteous and good acts done by ourselves, for ourselves or others, are to God an unclean rag. The vermin filled and pus stained rags of the leprous beggar is what we are in God's sight without Jesus Christ as our Savior. Christ changed all that when He healed our disease of sin and gave us new clothes of righteousness to be worn in the presence of the Father. That is a complete and fulfilled work of Christ that is unalterable forever. That is our position in heaven as fully described for us in the book of Hebrews.

But (isn't that a sad word) there is another reality. We don't live in heaven, we live on earth. On earth we keep getting dirty. That is why the perfect labor of Christ is so important. God sees us in Christ and our cleanness. We, on the other hand need to see ourselves in the reality of both worlds. We need to always remember that we are perfect in the Father's presence, but also that we are imperfect in this imperfect world. In this world we get dirty again and again.

We are sinners by birth and nature and the entire Bible points out to us that faith in Christ doesn't change that birth or natural inclination. We are still subject to the lust of the flesh and eyes and pride of life. We still have a natural man that wars against the spiritual man that is reborn in us. We still yield to temptations sore when we most desire not to do so. Paul speaks of himself in the present tense in Romans 7:19 "For the good that I will to do, I do not do: but the evil I will not to do, that I practice." Since Christ made clear in the Sermon on the Mount that sin is as much a matter of the heart as it is of the flesh, we must all find ourselves in the same position as Paul. We all sin. In fact to even say that we do not sin is a lie and therefore a sin. I John 1:8 says "If we say that we have no sin, we are a liar (or deceive ourselves), and the truth is not in us."

There we are – dirty again. But only dirty in the present reality and not in the heavenly one and we must remember that. So we need a bath. We need one badly and we need one daily. How do we get this bath? Paul says in Ephesians 5:26 that we are washed through the word. The word of God will show us the dirt in our lives and where it is located and what to wash. Jesus washed the disciples' feet and not their whole bodies and said to them that the whole body didn't need it. The body is clean forever through His once for all shed blood. Daily parts of it get dirty and need to be cleaned. How do we do that? I John 1:9 tells us "If we confess our sins He is faithful and just to forgive us our sins and to cleanse us from all unrighteousness." A picture on our desks of us at our best might remind us of how we appear before God in Christ and how we need to retain that appearance before man every day. It sure helps with Molly.

CHAPTER TWENTY

"The angel of the Lord encamps round about them that fear Him,
and delivers them."
Psalm 34:7

I hate to confuse the images portrayed in the various parables about Molly, but I must do so here. When she came to us she was "the devil dog." Unfortunately, some of my children have poor manners and still call her that. What of forgiveness, I ask, but all for naught. And so, alas for Molly, she must be recast for this parable into that terrible state in which she began.

Not only to some of my children is Molly still "Devil Dog", but to her great nemesis, the squirrel on the porch, she remains that way as well. Actually it is not just one squirrel. There is a whole family of them. Our porch is their playground. The flower pots on our porch are their hiding places for nuts. The corn and seeds strewn on the porch in the winter time is their dinner table. The nest in the big tree in front of our house is their home.

My bride and I like to watch them cavort about. The grandchildren like to watch them chase each other and tumble in the shrubs by the porch. They present a constant show of tumbling, acrobatics and aerobatics to all who want to watch for as long as anyone may wish to watch. But there is one who is not content to watch their sport with any appreciation – "Devil Dog".

We have two windows that look out onto the porch. In the living room is a side window to the bay window and that overlooks the porch from one end. In the kitchen is a tall window reaching to only 18 inches off the floor that looks directly onto the very center of the porch. The first thing in the morning that must be done is to open the curtains on those windows. If they are not pulled back, Molly is apt to pull them back with less grace than we might appreciate. She can see the squirrels right through the curtains and she reacts to what she sees.

Boy! Does she ever react to what she sees! She growls and barks and throws herself at the windows with abandon. I have given up trying to keep the woodwork on the bottom of the kitchen window painted. She strips it bare as her paws fly across the woodwork and hit against the glass. She digs and claws at the glass and has some very unsaintly moments. Then I have to intervene and say sharply, "Molly, stop it!" She wags her tail and goes and lies down in the other room until she thinks I am not watching anymore and then it is back to the window to watch for squirrels. Repeat above sequence *ad nauseum*.

Do you know what would be nice? I would like to take a picture of Molly in one of those cute poses with the dog and squirrel facing each other calmly through the glass pane of the window. What would be even nicer? How about one of those cute pictures of a dog and a squirrel lying peacefully together one on top of the other? Ah, friendship! Well, *it ain't agonna' happen!* Nope!

Molly is the resident hater of squirrels. She hates them with a vicious hatred. I am not sure why. I am not a dog psychologist and I am not biblically inclined to place much faith in dog psychologists either. Perhaps I could see it if she just let her tail twitch a little like the cats' tails do when they watch the birds and utter a soft growl. That would be an acceptable response.

But, no, she goes crazy. She HATES squirrels. She roars out her hatred and seeks their destruction. You see, she is the "Devil Dog".

Satan hates us. It is not a casual dislike. Satan hates God, but he can't get at God. It's not that he hasn't tried. He rose up in rebellion against God somewhere in time past and got the boot out of his esteemed position as chief archangel of heaven. What he can't do to God, he has opted to do to man. He will hurt man, the special creation of God, the only creation made in God's image, and thereby fling back his hatred at God. Satan is not shy about his hatred. He has thrown himself relentlessly at man since the Garden of Eden.

In the Garden God had told man that in the day he ate of the tree of the knowledge of good and evil that he would die. What did Satan tempt Eve to eat? He went after her with the fruit of that tree because then she and Adam would die. They would DIE! That was his goal. He hated God and hates man. Instead, God's grace was poured out and He killed an animal instead of them and covered them with the bloody skins to show the way of the future sacrifice of His own Son for man's sin and rebellion.

In the process of time Satan has cast every imaginable and repugnant temptation in front of man and man has happily lapped it up. He is trying to make man so odious to God that He will have to destroy us in His utter frustration. Satan is too blinded by his hatred of man to understand the amazing love of God for His special creation and His wonderful grace to usward through His beloved Son. And so, Satan still throws himself fanatically against man. Jesus says of Satan that he is a thief and that he comes not but to steal and to kill and to destroy. (John 10:10)

Certainly Satan likes to kill God's children. From Pharaoh's persecutions in 1500BC to the great communist and Islamic assaults against Christians that have killed and keep on killing over 100 million born again Christians in the 20th and 21st centuries, Satan has been busy killing the people that he hates so much. Satan hates God and God's people. We must never forget it. But he acts out his hatred in other ways as well.

Another Satanic plan of attack against those who trust in Christ as Savior is the name given to him in Scripture. In Revelation 13:10 Satan is called the "accuser of the brethren". He is barking at us all the time. He barks at us before the very throne of God. We see him engaged in this activity in Job chapters one and two. He is always busy bringing charges against us before God. (Let us be clear here that Satan is not omnipresent, he cannot see all that we do or know all that we think. Only God can do that.) Satan's charges are not necessarily specific. They are aimed at the general state of man as sinful and they often come from the suppositions of his own evil nature. That is clear from the accusation that he made against Job. They were not founded on anything other than the very evil nature of himself and how he would react in Job's position. But there he is anyway, accusing the brethren, born again believers, of sin against God.

But wait! Yes, just like the infomercials on TV - there's more. Not only is there more, but there is more that is better. Satan is like Molly barking at the glass. She can't get to the squirrels. There is a barrier between her and them and there is a barrier between Satan and us. We are in Christ. Christ is the barrier. He sits at the right hand of the Father and pleads His shed blood on our behalf. No, He says, they are not guilty, they are perfect in Me. Praise God for this glorious barrier!

Being in Christ is a simple illustration. Take a shatterproof and bullet proof glass jar. That jar is Christ. When we believe in Jesus, we literally are placed in Christ, that totally secure jar. God's hand guards the top of the jar and lets in all who come to Christ by faith and He keeps them in the jar until we spend future eternity with Him. Satan can bark all he wants around the outside of that jar, but it doesn't hurt us any at all.

Satan also is busy accusing us to ourselves. He makes us

know just how unfit we are to be called by the precious name of Jesus. He howls at us of our unworthiness and throws the mud of guilt at us more than any seen in a political campaign. He scratches and claws at the jar to make us cringe in self-deprecation. But the jar holds. We are not to listen to his accusations. We are to hear Christ's promises. We are, of course, to confess known sins, but we must then accept as the gift of God that those sins have been removed and forgotten by our Father. There is no condemnation for those who are in Christ Jesus, Paul tells us in Romans 8, and we are to trust in God's word and not in the vile words of Satan. We often hear him barking through the glass, but the strength of Christ so overwhelms him that all Satan can do is howl. Let us feed contently in the presence of our Lord who keeps His own and loses not one sheep of His fold or squirrel of His porch.

That window in the kitchen is a new, solid, double paned window that isn't going to give way to Molly's attacks against the squirrels. They are secure and mostly they know it and ignore her. When Satan accuses us the accusation is deflected by Christ. We need to see the jar and rejoice. We need not get burdened with accusations but rejoice in the Savior. When Satan actually has a true accusation, and we give him plenty of opportunity to do so, then we need to confess and receive the cleansing and continued assurance of our safe retreat in Christ.

Molly hates the squirrels and Satan hates us. Between both there is a barrier of protection. Let us praise God for the safety of His Son.

CHAPTER TWENTY-ONE

"And let us consider one another to provoke..."
Hebrews 10:24

Like a small child, Molly's life mostly revolves around herself and her immediate family. That would be primarily my beloved bride and me. But there are also others that interact with her and contribute to her life and the available examples for parables. There are the two resident cats at our house and there are two dogs with which she has the most frequent interaction. How do these animals play out in the drama of Christian experience? What lessons are derived from their characters? Do their personalities make a passage of Scripture become clearer? Their approaches to life, simple animal life, certainly make some clear statements of profound truth.

The least frequent visitor to our house and Molly's least liked acquaintance is Sadie. Sadie is our son's wife's parent's resident dog. If our son and his wife are dog sitting for Sadie, they will bring her over here if they come. Sadie is an English Springer spaniel. She is the younger sister to Drake, our son's resident dog. She is about two years old and not a very big dog for her breed, being only about half the size of Molly.

We all know people that we would rather not have come for a visit. Each of us would have a different reason for not wanting that particular person to stop in and sit a while. Sadie is Molly's "person" that she doesn't look forward to seeing. The reason is simple; Sadie is a provoker.

As a pastor for many years I know quite well that there are people in the church who truly believe that provocation is their spiritual gift. They are sure that the proverb, "As iron sharpens iron, so man sharpens man" is the actual work that God has given them to do in this world. They are the sharpeners and everyone else needs sharpening. They are the ones who see your mistakes, real or perceived, and must correct them. They are the advice givers without waiting for a request for their advice.

I thought that Sadie just liked to provoke Molly, but that is not so. Our son says that Sadie finds the same work to do at their house in provoking Drake. She wants to provoke Drake to the work of greater patience by taking his toys and then shaking them in his face. "Ha, ha; you need to learn to share. I will provoke you to learn that lesson." If it is not a toy then it is jumping up into an already occupied lap and kicking the other dog off. Of course, she then barks at the displaced dog and wags her stumpy little tail. Whatever the other dogs are doing she will jump in and disrupt and then get into their face. If Sadie had a finger you know she would be wagging it and making her statement that there was an important lesson to be learned and she was God's appointed teacher.

Provokers are not generally very popular and don't know why not. If they have a mission to do, why doesn't everyone appreciate it? Provokers can be very judgmental and say, "Oh, those people just don't want to grow. They are content in their unspiritual lives." I know all this because provokers talk to pastors and they are very sincere in their confusion about their role and other peoples' responses to it.

How do we respond to the irksome provocation of these people with their misguided missions? Drake won't attack Sadie. He will get frustrated and bark at her and get down in an aggressive position, but he won't attack. Those would be responses quite a bit like many humans take. They get in a defensive stance when the provoker comes around and try to talk without saying anything that could possibly bring about further provocation. They talk and talk and keep the conversation innocuous and shallow. It is a safe retreat.

Molly has a different response. She moves the first time or goes to find another toy the first time, but then she reacts. Molly will rip into Sadie and go after her fang and claw. She will only pursue that course for about five seconds until she has driven Sadie away, and then she calms down and takes back whatever Sadie took. This, of course, leads to a predictable response from Sadie. She comes back to take it again. She is a provoker. The lesson must be learned by the provokee or else it must be retaught. This cycle soon gets old and Molly gets put in the back yard and has no clue why.

Molly's response is also not uncommon in churches. People will get fed up with the provoker and often say nasty and hurtful things to them. The result, however, is that the provoker is only more certain of that person's spiritual need to get right that it leads to a cycle of frustration for all. People leave churches out of frustration. (It is never the provokers that go.) Other people have no idea why the break of fellowship occurred and the whole body suffers from the repeated incidents.

Bump, one of our resident cats has a third response. When Sadie comes over he just jumps into the clothes basket on the dryer and stays out of the way. Avoidance is the easiest course to take. This is a common course in churches as well. We walk around people and ignore them. It is safe and easy.

Drake, Molly, Bump and Sadie are all dogs and cats and cannot reason any of this out. Each has their own temperament and that is how things will go. Sadie provokes. Drake barks. Molly attacks. Bump avoids. Repeat the cycle again and again. With people it can be different.

First, there is no point in trying to get the provoker not to provoke. It is not that they don't know the last half of the verse in Hebrews, (to love one another) they do. Their goal is to get others to love more and do more good works. The love and good works will, of course, be at the discretion and judgment of the provoker. Unless and until God gets a hold of their hearts and teaches them the truth, they will not hear it or learn it from man. A spiritual calling is a spiritual calling after all, no matter how much they harm the church.

Is there another option of response to provokers? What I want to do is simply say to them is, "Who died and made you God?" I don't. But I really, really want to. People say to me, "You are a pastor, so of course you can't say that." My answer is always the same, "Is the laity excused from acting with biblical decorum and only the pastor obligated to do so?" For a moment I get to be the biblical provoker. (Anything said with genuine love and a smile on one's face can account for a lot of successful provocation.)

My approach to the provoker is to try to sincerely treat them as family. If we went to a family reunion and Uncle George was always making provocative comments, we would just love him and say, "Well, that's Uncle George." Uncle George would not be left sitting alone at the table. He is family after all.

Christ says that we are a family. The slacker, the ne'er do well, the over achiever, the ditz and Uncle George are all family. We too often lose sight of our relationship with others in Jesus Christ. They are our brothers and sisters. We will be living all eternity with them. We know that in eternity all their rough edges will be shaved off in the perfection of our bodies, but so will our rough edges. Every person who has trusted Christ as Savior, whether or not they are our same race, creed, temperament, social standing or intellectual equal, are all family. They are our brothers and sisters by a greater blood tie than those of our own earthly clan. We have been bought and paid for with them by the precious blood of Christ and in Him we are one.

Still, and honestly, there are family members that we are glad to only see at reunions and we don't want them around every day. That is a natural response, but not a very spiritual one. I know, it isn't easy and I don't pretend that it is. What we need is to be more open to what God is trying to teach us.

The provoker is all wrong. They are trying to take the place of God in rubbing off the rough edges of fellow believers. The passage in Hebrews clearly is not pointing in that direction. We should encourage others to love and good works. The King James word "provoke" has lost some of its luster in modern parlance. While the provoker is all wrong, God is not. He is always all right.

God wants to round us off to reflect His image. What the provoker wants is irrelevant. God wants us to love. So, we must love the provoker. We must see him or her as family and accept them. We can't change Uncle George and we can't change the provoker in the pew next to us. We can only work on letting God change us. God allows provokers, not so that we will listen to them, but so that we will listen to Him. He wants to mold us into His image and make us vessels of His grace to others. We can't escape people with rude problems in the world, so we must learn to rightly deal with them in the church. As we grow in the grace of God toward those who most annoy us in church, we can grow as extenders of grace to those who are ungodly outside the church.

Sadie can't really change. She is a dog. Molly and Drake will always respond how they respond because they are dogs, too. We aren't dogs. We are God's children who provoked His rightful wrath day after day by our sins. He still sent His Son to love us and make us part of His family. In Christ, we must learn to do the same.

CHAPTER TWENTY-TWO

"Shall we receive good at the hand of God, and shall we
not receive evil?"
Job 2:10

While Sadie is certainly Molly's greatest antagonist, her brother Drake is by far Molly's best friend. If our son happens to come to our house without Drake, Molly will go to the window and whine. She will run to the back door to see if Drake is coming in that way instead. If Drake doesn't appear she will whine some more and chase from door to door in search of her friend. Finally she will mope. She wants her playmate.

Drake also likes Molly. That is helpful since unrequited love would be sad in a dog. But Drake is very friendly to Molly and likes to chase and play with her. Add those two playing together to six grandchildren running around the house and we have quite a circus sometimes.

Drake isn't just a playmate of Molly's though. He is a hard working dog. Our son likes to hunt and Drake is a good hunting dog. While he likes to sleep at the foot of our son and his wife's king sized bed, he also likes to tramp through the fields in search of pheasants. He is well trained and responsible both at home and in the field. But life hasn't always been easy for Drake.

Three years ago Drake encountered a great tragedy in his life. Vandals broke into our son's house and destroyed everything. They carved up countertops, poured solvents into electrical appliances, poured paint on the carpets, smashed china, cut up the walls, destroyed albums and important records kept in files and essentially destroyed anything and everything in the home. They did not, however, stop with those acts of vandalism. They captured Drake and tortured him severely. The vet didn't know if Drake would survive.

The great question that has been asked for millennia is, "Why do bad things happen to good people?" God gives us the book of Job to explain things a little. It is because of things we don't see, know or could possibly understand. Bad things happen and there is one common response – anger towards God. Job was uncommon in his response which makes his response such an important teaching tool.

Job didn't get angry with God. Now, Job's wife told him that he should. She gave the common response. In thirty years of pastoral ministry I have heard the common response given time after time. "If God cared about me then this wouldn't have happened to me. I can't really care about a God who would let this happen to me. If God wants my loyalty, He needs to be more loyal to me." Those are angry words from people who are angry with God.

Along with angry words comes a pitiful life of barren religiosity. People attend church to show God up. "I am still here, God, even though You weren't there for me." They are indeed still there in body, but their spirit is far from the pew and the altar. It is nearly impossible to get people who are angry with God to commit to any real work of grace for God or for His church. Angry and arrogant compliance is sometimes offered, but no work of grace.

Still others, perhaps far more, just "give up" on God. They stop attending church and spew their anger to any who will hear. Pastors and Christian workers call on their home only to hear a litany of God's failures. They feel rightly justified in turning their backs on the God who turned His back on them in their time of grief or need. They don't "need" a God who can't come up with the goods on an on demand basis. They are bitter to man and bitter to God.

Then there was Job. God had allowed Satan to take his possessions, his wealth, his health, his children and all his hope in this life. But Job didn't give up his hope in God. He said, "The Lord gave and the Lord hath taken away. Blessed be the Name of the Lord." (1:21) Job wanted to die, but in death he still expected to see God and be welcomed by Him. Job had a great response to adversity.

Drake has had a great response to adversity. Drake has gotten on with his life and lives it well. He continues to have confidence in his master and is obedient in following his master's will. He survived through the first night after his ordeal and then got on with what dogs get on with. Oh, yes, Drake is a little more cautious of strangers. He will take a defensive stand in uncertain circumstances. But, he doesn't keep it up. A touch of the master's hand or a word of the master's voice and Drake is back in balance with life.

It is a certainty that every day of our life will not be filled with sunshine. Roses will have thorns. The calamities of the world will befall the believer as much as they will befall the lost. Factories that employ believers will close as quickly as factories that employ only the lost. Flu epidemics will not follow the pattern of the death angel on Passover. The house of the believer will have a star placed in the window for a fallen soldier son or daughter the same as the house of the lost.

Wouldn't it be great if it were not so? Then everyone would flock to Jesus Christ, not as the needed Savior of their lost soul, but as the insurance policy against natural and manmade disasters. Is that all Jesus is, an insurance policy? When Jesus fed the 5000 and they tried to make Him their king, He withdrew from them. They wanted the world for themselves and He wanted heaven for them. He didn't come to insure a full pantry, He came to save sinners. Our response to adversity is a work of grace in His grand outreach to sinful man.

Paul writes to the Corinthians, "Blessed be the God and Father of our Lord Jesus Christ, the Father of mercies and God of all comfort who comforts us in all our tribulation, that we may comfort those who are in any trouble, with the comfort with which we ourselves are comforted by God." (II Corinthians 1:3-4) What does Paul say? Does He say that God is a cad for allowing us to experience pain and suffering? No, he says that God is the God of all mercy and comfort. How do we know that He is the God of all mercy and comfort? We know it because in this world we will experience all manner of trials and tribulations and God will be there in His great mercy to comfort us.

Is there a purpose in His comforting us? Yes, it is twofold. First He comforts us because He loves us. As any father would show mercy to a hurting child and hold them in love, so He shows mercy to us and holds us in His loving arms. That human fathers often fail at this task does not mean for a moment that the Great Heavenly Father also fails to do so. No, He promises to do so and He keeps all His promises. God is all manner of great things: Justice, Holy, Pure, Vengeful, Almighty, but in it all He is still the God of love. Every single attribute listed encompasses His love.

Secondly God comforts us to enable us to comfort others. An entire Amish family was killed when a man ran into their buggy with his car. The driver of the car was also killed. The Amish family's relatives took food baskets to the family of the driver of the car. They knew that the wife and children would be in need at the loss of the husband and father. That is the meaning of God giving us comfort that we might also comfort those who are in any trouble in this world.

When the world doesn't see an angry response toward God when we experience adversity, it wants to know why. Our proper response to the adversities of life are far more effective in speaking to the world about God's grace than if we simply try to sell Him as the great insurance policy against all ills. Men sorrow at the ills of life and the losses those ills bring. Paul tells us to sorrow not like them without hope, but to sorrow with the hope of Christ. Sorrowing with hope gives a testimony to the lost world that Christ makes a real difference.

A Christ that promises no calamities would be an unreal Christ. A real Christ aids us in dealing with a real world. Real people will want to know more about a real Christ than a plastic model that has no substance. There are preachers, of course, who try to peddle an "Insurance Policy Christ", but they are all charlatans. Christ told His followers that they would experience tribulation in this world. Paul told those same followers that it is our response to these tribulations that make us effective ministers of the God of grace who saved us and sustains us.

Bad things happen. There are two responses. We can take the common road and blame God. We can take the Christian road and accept God's comfort and then spread that comfort around to others.

Drake had a horrible experience. It truly nearly killed him. He is still alive, and that means he has choices how to react. He has reacted with confidence in his master and obedience to his master. He is calmed by his master's hand and voice. Because of his good conduct and response, Drake is a great friend both for and to Molly. Molly's life would be emptier without Drake's input. Other's lives can be fuller because of our response to Christ, our Master, in our adversity as well.

CHAPTER TWENTY-THREE

"Let each of you look out not only for his own interests, but also for the interests of others."
Philippians 2:4

When Molly became our resident dog, we already had two cats. Bump has been around our house for fifteen years and Smokey for eleven. Molly was not well acquainted with cats before she came here. The cats have revealed a trait in Molly that is exceptional; she is the eternal optimist. Molly thinks she can herd cats. In four years of living with them it has never occurred to her that cats don't want to be herded. She just keeps on trying. Bump and Smokey take entirely different responses to this activity. But it is Smokey's response that helps to illustrate a parable.

Smokey's response to Molly is a great deal like Smokey's response to almost anything. Smokey is an indifferent cat in general, but she is particularly quick to pull up stakes if something is expected of her. Smokey can and does ignore Molly with the greatest of ease almost all the time. But, when Molly really wants to play "herd the cats", Smokey abandons her indifference and finds a new warm spot to lie in. Smokey, in short, will not participate in the games of others.

Smokey has the attitude so common in our society; look out

for *numero uno* first! This is the attitude of the world since the Garden of Eden. Satan lied to Eve and told her that God was trying to rip her off. God was holding back on the good stuff and if Eve knew what was good for her, she should grab for it. Eve bit and Adam bit along with her and the process of grasping for our own benefit first sprung into the human condition. When God called their actions into question they were quick to defend themselves and blame others – including God.

God calls for the people who call upon His Name to think in a different vein. He wants us to put the considerations of others before our consideration for our self. The big question of "What's in it for me" is not to be our big question. Our big question is to be, "How can I help you?" That question is not in Smokey's think tank.

Smokey likes service. She likes to lie in front of the heat vent. She likes to lie on a warm lap. She likes to push her way first to the food bowl. She likes to, cry at the door to go out and as soon as she is out she likes to cry at the door to come back in. (Actually she jumps up on a stand by the kitchen window and bats the window to get back in.) Smokey is demanding and self-centered. Smokey is not a mouser and she doesn't like to play with Molly and she doesn't particularly like to play with Bump. If my beloved bride or I are reading a book, she likes to jump in our laps and get in the way of the book. She is an exceedingly beautiful cat and that is the sole actual basis of her worth. (She does have value in that our youngest daughter did bring her home and asked to keep her and that makes her special in any kind of sentimental way.) In short, Smokey likes to look out for Smokey and no one else.

On the road up to Jerusalem, James and John came to Jesus and asked to sit on His right hand and left hand in the Kingdom. Jesus corrected their wrong attitude with an unexpected one, at least for them. He told them that the greatest would be the servant of all, not lord it over all. Paul echoes that sentiment in Philippians chapter two where he tells us not to be looking out for ourselves, but to look out for others. What a contradictory thought for man? It is calling us out of the comfort of our sinful condition to be something that we naturally are not.

Let us consider the proposition. Jesus is to be Lord of all. He is to have the preeminence as Paul tells the Colossians. In other words, Jesus is to be number one. It is not a position He is to share with us or anyone else. That prospect places us as number two in the scheme of things. But we don't rate that high in God's scheme of things. God tells us to put others before ourselves. If we do that then we fall to number 3. Who are we to please first? God. Who are we to help next? Others. Who are we to consider last? Ourselves.

This doesn't sound much like the modern church. Here is what is heard over and over again. We just can't keep going to this church — it doesn't meet our needs. There are few other more self-serving or self-centered comments than that. It flies in the very face of what Christ has commanded and what Paul has enjoined. Service isn't our motto, but being served is our expectation. "The music ministry doesn't serve our needs." "The children's ministry doesn't serve our needs." "The unpadded pews don't serve our needs." For every one person in the church who asks how they can serve, there are ten or more who are ready to pull up stakes if they don't think they are being adequately served.

Jesus' call to be like Him, who came not to be served but to serve, is becoming unfashionable in contemporary Christianity. My daughter attends an evangelical church of over 400 members. When the call went out for Sunday school teachers for the junior department there wasn't a single volunteer. (On my daughter's behalf she is already teaching the primaries.) An area missionary spoke in eleven churches to a total of more than one thousand people to raise workers for Bible clubs in public schools. There were a total of twenty-six people who responded to the call and only half were still involved in the ministry two years later.

In the book of Ecclesiastes wise king Solomon said, "Whatever your hand finds to do, do it with all your might". His advice presupposes that people are looking for something to do with their hands. Too many hands are idle and too many people are looking to be served instead of serving. In Matthew 24 Jesus counsels the wise servant to be busy serving when Christ comes. He has a dire warning for the slothful servant but a generous promise for the busy one.

First of all I know that we all live in a busy time, but that cannot become a primary excuse for disobedience to God. Our grandparents lived in a day when the work week was sixty hours long. There were no microwave ovens to quickly zap a dinner and very few restaurants in which to eat out. Money was in short supply and few could eat out if they wanted to do so. Meals were largely made from scratch by wives and mothers who didn't have automatic clothes washers and dryers. The dryers were long lines in the back yard. The vast majority of today's "labor saving" devices hadn't even been invented yet. Food was canned from a big backyard garden.

In those busy days Sunday school teachers were not hard to find. It was considered an honor to work for the Lord. The area missionary seeking workers for Bible clubs had over 70 weekly workers reaching boys and girls for Christ in our city. In those busy days it was not thought to be a task but an opportunity to be used of God in a servant's role. In those busy days when work was longer and harder for everyone in the family, people seldom changed churches to be served but were busy serving in the churches where they attended.

In his inaugural address in 1961 John Kennedy said that we were not to ask what our country could do for us, but what we could do for our country. That challenge resonated across a generation of people who wanted to line up for service of any kind to help the people around them and the nation that they loved. Today we need the same call to go out from our pulpits. Ask not what your church can do for you, but what you can do for your church. We need a clear understanding that God has called us to serve and not to be served.

From the inception of the church the record of history is that the church was a servant to mankind. Earliest writings tell of believers who would pick up abandoned babies thrown out by the side of the road and give them a home. Early Christian apologists, when arguing with secular debaters of their age, would mark out clearly the territory of service provided by the persecuted church to the overall welfare of the community that was persecuting them. Serving was synonymous with being a Christian. It is what Jesus said should be synonymous with being a Christian.

Smokey is not a good team player. She isn't into caring for others. She is all about caring for herself. Smokey adds nothing essential to our house but window dressing. I have a soft spot for her because she was a stray that needed a home and she is sentimentally attached through my daughter's affection for her. There are many Christians these days just like her. They have found a home in Christ away from the cold and starvation of the world and they are loved by the pastor for Christ's sake, but they are of no essential value to the church of Jesus Christ or the advancement of the Gospel. This simply should not be so. We all need to look in the mirror and see if Smokey is looking back at us. If so we need to amend our ways before God and man and seek to have the master find us diligently working for Him when He comes again.

CHAPTER TWENTY-FOUR

"And forgive us our debts, as we forgive our debtors."
Matthew 6:12

Molly's favorite doggy friend is Drake, but he is not her best friend. That special distinction goes to our other resident cat, Bump. Bump has been with us for fifteen years. He came to us by private adoption from a farm family. His name reflects his experience and his character.

Bump got his name from tragedy. Bump was attacked by a pack of loose dogs that came to the farmyard where he lived. He was literally eaten up. His body was torn up and his insides were on the outside. But before Bump died he was rescued by the farmer and taken to the vet. The vet put the inside back on the inside and said he didn't know if it would work or not. It did. The name Bump comes from the bump he had in his life. The farmer took Bump home and kept him inside for several months to heal. While inside the house Bump became attached to the house dogs of the farmer. Instead of holding the vicious assault against dogs in general, Bump "forgave" dogkind and learned to live in love and harmony with them. Fearing for Bump's safety if he were returned to the barnyard, the farmer sought a good home for him and we were it.

When Molly came to live with us, Smokey ran and hid on the

top of the kitchen cupboards. Bump stood his ground. He didn't hiss or spit. He just stood his ground. He looked at Molly while Molly danced around like the devil dog she was known to be and stood his ground. Molly would bounce at Bump in jerky leaps, but Bump just stood his ground. Molly's most devilish behavior did not perturb Bump. It was a battle of wills and Molly lost. In reality, though, she gained. She gained the best friend she has, a cat who lives out the reality of forgiveness.

Molly needs a lot of forgiveness. Cat herding is actually rather hard on the cat. Molly gets the cat by the neck and carries him to the desired place. The cat now has matted fur soaked in dog slobber. With one cat deposited in the desired place Molly goes off to get the other one. Only once or twice has she ever gotten Smokey, and then forgiveness was not the word to be employed. By this time, however, Bump has run off to lie comfortably in the place of his choice and the game begins again.

Jesus talked about forgiving our brother seventy times seven. Most people that I know stop short of the original seven that Peter asked for. That number seemed like a lot to Peter and it seems like a lot to most others as well. The response usually is, "Well, if they had been truly sorry it wouldn't have happened again, so why should I forgive them again?" The thought always comes to me, how many times are we truly sorry that we have offended God, but it happens again. God forgives us more than seventy times seven. Bump has forgiven Molly her full seventy times seven with many to spare.

How is it clear that he has forgiven Molly? I have a big chair, big enough to hold at least three grandchildren. That is plenty big to hold two pets. Molly likes to sit in my lap. Bump likes to sit in my lap. The happy outcome is that they both will sit in my lap together. Bump will bathe Molly and then Molly will bathe Bump. It is a regular love fest and I am its happy location.

Churches are to be love fests. It should constantly be said of Christians, "My, how they love one another." It should be said, but it isn't said nearly as often as it should. What keeps us from love? Quite often it is the lack of forgiveness. We let incidences from our past guide our present and ruin our future.

At some moment in the past, perhaps at some moment of great personal vulnerability, someone tripped us in the center aisle of the church, so to speak. It was not a private injury to our pride or mind or body. To us it was a major and very public event of grievous intent by ill hearted and callous beings. It matters not to us that everyone's head was bowed in prayer and no one else knows about it. It came at a point when we needed a helping hand and instead we got tossed on our face. The hurt that it generated is all out of proportion to the exact incident, but since the hurt is personal no one else really understands how much it has torn into us.

As a pastor I am acutely aware of the pitfalls that can generate this kind of hurt. A name forgotten on a list of volunteers can rend the heart of the one ignored. Sometimes it can be overlooked and made up. Sometimes, however, the one overlooked is going through a time of personal difficulty and the accidental slight becomes a deliberate assault on their self-worth. I have personally escaped retribution for this kind of incident, but I know of a man who lost his job over it. I have known those who have been hurt to quit the church over the incident. Hurt is very real.

Since hurt is very real, forgiveness must also be very real. If forgiveness doesn't become real, then the hurt worms its way to the center of our being and like any harmful parasite it begins to eat away at the core of the tree. At the start the evidence of the disease can be very minimal. An occasional sad face may replace a generally happy countenance. A little less warmth in a greeting or a little withdrawal from the offending party with whom the hurt individual used to be close may take place. Gradually the damage of the parasite grows. Then it becomes a full blown disease and the remedy is more difficult to arrive at because the cause is cased in obscurity.

In the Lord's Prayer, Jesus calls upon us to understand the need for personal forgiveness. He says pray, "Forgive us our debts." This is a call to see and know that we are imperfect people ourselves. We offend God and most often think little or nothing of it. It is not that we are deliberately callous toward God; we just aren't sensitive to Him. He has asked us to love Him above all things. That is an impossibility on a day to day plane. He loses first place to our jobs, our families, our daily lives. It is clear that every day we should pray, "Forgive me for not loving You as fully as I should". And will God forgive us? Certainly He will.

Just this one illustration shows us our need for forgiveness. We need it daily and soon we will have far surpassed seventy times seven. If we need and receive daily forgiveness on just this one point, the greatness of our need and the all surpassing greatness of His grace and love become more real to us. As the reality of our need and His forgiveness is brought alive in our lives, then we understand the second half of this part of the prayer.

"As we forgive our debtors," is the part we don't want to forget. Daily, daily, daily, God forgives because we need it. Daily we need something else. The joy that we receive at the forgiveness of God can be multiplied in our lives as we daily forgive others. If we don't like carrying around the load of our own sin, why should we want to carry around the load of someone else's sin? Often it wasn't even a sin to begin with. It was an accident, a non-deliberate oversight, a chance foul-up that could happen to anyone or some other situation that the offending party doesn't even know about. What has happened to that innocent start is that it has become a sin to us as we have nursed it along. Now we bear the load of someone else's sin. How unhappy are we?

The joy of the Lord and the joy of the fellowship of His saints have been robbed from us. They have been robbed from us by ourselves. We seek forgiveness and joy, but we cannot be forgiven for their sin. We have to do the forgiving. We flip it around in our prayers and ask God to forgive us for not forgiving them and then get back to fellowship with both God and man. The Bible gives a process of resolving this if your brother knows that he has offended you. Go to him and say I forgive you. Many times, though, the offender is entirely in the dark because offense was never intended or an action was not even known to have taken place. Here we can exorcise that destroying worm of anger with prayer. "Lord, forgive me for carrying this burden and I forgive whomever it was that I blame for the hurt that I feel." When Satan plays Sadie the provoker and reminds us of our hurt, we simply breathe the prayer again, "Lord, it is forgiven."

Forgiveness is more fun than nursing anger and hurt. Bump is a good example. He could forever be angry at the dogs that tore him apart. He could apply that anger to all other dogs as well. But, where would be the fun in that? Bump loves to play and Molly is a good playmate. Bump loves to be affectionate, and Molly loves to reciprocate affection. If Bump "chose" not to "forgive", and these words are in quotes because it is an animal we are talking about, then he would be a lonely cat with only uncooperative Smokey as a companion for most of the day. Many believers are just like that. They are lonely and unfulfilled in their Christian lives. They need to take a lesson from Bump, "As we forgive our debtors." The blessings of the joy of God will be poured out on all who do so.

CHAPTER TWENTY-FIVE

"You shall teach them diligently to your children, and shall talk of them when you sit in your house, when you walk by the way, when you lie down and when you rise up."
Deuteronomy 6:7

Molly doesn't factor in this chapter; we do. We who are children of our loving heavenly Father, who are called by His Name, who are unspeakably precious to Him, we have been charged by Him to place Him at the forefront of our thoughts at all times. We are to remember Him when we sit down, rise up and do everything in our daily routine in between. To do this we must see God in our lives, in our surroundings, in His creation and in the situations that confront us. We can find pictures of Him in our families, our pets, our working relationships, our church relationships and on and on. In fact, we must find Him there or we will miss the beauty and glory of all those things that God brings into our lives to see and know Him better.

Our wonderful God is not far off. He is near. He is close at hand. He isn't, as the pagan would say, in the tree. But He did make the tree. He is illustrated in its many facets. He used a tree to illustrate the doom of Nebuchadnezzar. He used a fruitless tree to illustrate the doom of unbelievers. Trees can become tremendous tools for teaching about both God and man. When we see a tree we can either see a large plant with branches or we can see illustrations of God and of God working with men. God lays the groundwork for this type of association clearly in His word. It is with these simple tools that we stay connected in our daily lives to God's wonderful care for us and His great expectations of His children.

In Matthew chapter 13 Jesus gave a number of parables. In those parables he discussed people at work. He talked about the animal kingdom and the plant kingdom. He spoke of finances and the aspirations and dreams of man. He told of trouble and apparent disappointment. He took situation after situation from the commonness of life and transformed it in to great lessons about God.

In Romans chapter 1 Paul talks about the natural order of things revealing God to everyone's eyes. His creation reveals His glory. The psalmists of Israel would use this as a common theme to manifest the greatness of God. "The heavens declare the glory of God", they said. Indeed it is undisputable that God has revealed Himself in what He made. It is such a certainty that Paul says in Romans 1:20 that those who ignore the evidence of His created world are "without excuse."

Simply put, the commonness of life and the grandeur of creation give us ample source material to remember God at all times. That is what "The Gospel According to Molly" has been all about. It doesn't stop with my dog. It enters into the homes and lives of every believer. We all need to look and see the grace of God in the simplicity of our lives. He is there with us, caring for us, loving us, nurturing us and He wants to be seen and known as active. He wants us to be able to multiply our thankfulness to Him as we see Him relevant to who we are.

Theologians can write high sounding books about the nature and greatness of God. Those books may all be true, but they miss a point. We don't live in theology books. We live in homes and families and neighborhoods. We live with real people who rub against us in real ways. We know the proverb is true that states that as iron sharpens iron, so man sharpens man. We get rather sharper than we want sometimes.

It is in this nitty-gritty of life that we see God at work. Molly awakened me to a new appreciation of this. From devil dog to adopted family member, she showed me a wonderful work of grace in simple terms. I didn't think it through before any of it happened. It became clear as an afterthought. It was a lesson and it made me appreciate God all the more for my redemption. She first became a learning point for me of my own walk with God, and then a teaching point as I shared these things with others.

Each life will contain different learning points. We are to look for them. Then we are to teach them. Children relate easily to these simple illustrations. God tells us to teach them to our children. We don't have to force feed them theology books. We gently show them the wonders of God in the simple things. We see His grace and mercy more clearly when it is practical. Children will understand and make a connection with the God who is real. They will come to know Him as the One who is not far off.

Moses reminds us to make this a generational objective. We need to keep the lessons coming to those God brings to us as life goes along. In Deuteronomy 4:9 he says, "And teach them to your children and your grandchildren." The psalmist Asaph adds to this in Psalm 78:6, "That the generation to come might know them (the works of God), that the children who would be born, that they may arise and declare them to their children." The teaching process goes on and on and it must be made clear to the children to come. God is real. God is caring. God can be made ever present in our lives.

To this wonderful God we give thanks for His grace and mercy. We give thanks for His daily care. To help this all be more real to us, we need to look daily at what He brings our way and find Him active in it. God bless you in your journey of discovering always the presence of God in your life.

You can contact David at www.davidccraig.net

David Craig's Books

Made in the USA
San Bernardino, CA
27 March 2014